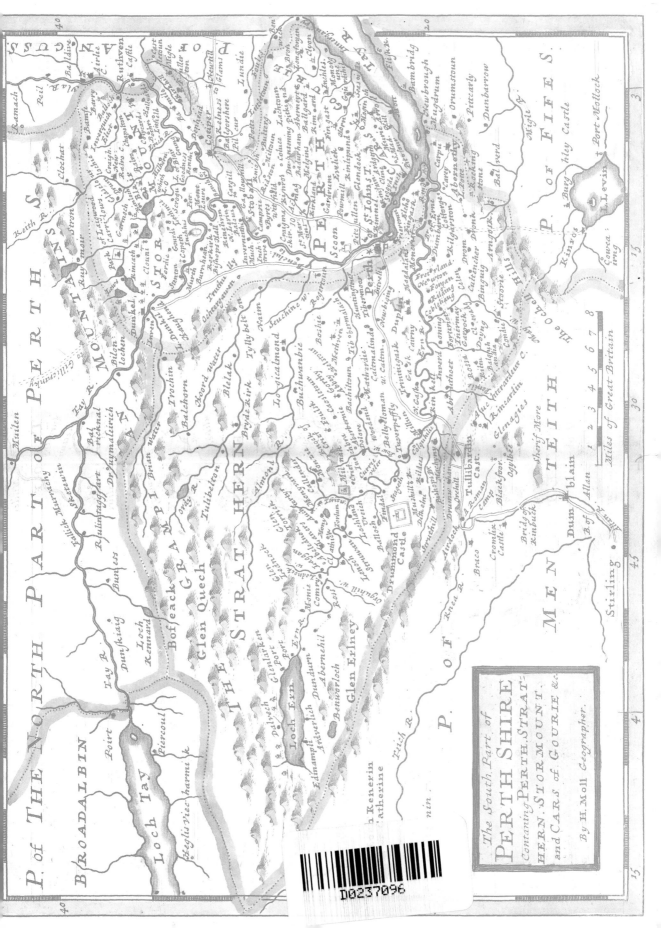

The South Part of
PERTH SHIRE
Containing PERTH, STRAT=
HERN. STORMOUNT.
and CARS of GOURIE &c.

By H. Moll Geographer.

Miles of Great Britain
1 2 3 4 5 6 7 8

THE RIVER TAY
AND ITS PEOPLE

THE
RIVER TAY
AND ITS PEOPLE

GRAHAM OGILVY

Photography by
GRAHAM McGIRK

Additional Photography by
ALAN RICHARDSON and **PERTHSHIRE TOURIST BOARD**

MAINSTREAM
PUBLISHING

EDINBURGH AND LONDON

In memory of Harry Ogilvy

First published in Great Britain in 1993 by
MAINSTREAM PUBLISHING COMPANY
(EDINBURGH) LTD
7 Albany Street
Edinburgh EH1 3UG

ISBN 1 85158 406 4

A catalogue record for this book is available from the British Library

Typeset in Great Britain by Saxon Graphics Ltd, Derby
Printed in Italy by New Interlitho, Milan

CONTENTS

INTRODUCTION

The idea for this book came with the return of RRS *Discovery* to Dundee. Along with other journalists, I was privileged to be taken out to the estuary to witness the vessel's historic return to its home port.

The Tay estuary presented a fantastic vista and inspired me to undertake my own journey of discovery to explore an area that I thought I knew well. The result is *The River Tay and Its People* which, I hope, will encourage visitors and locals alike to discover the charms of some of Britain's finest countryside. This book can only offer a glimpse of the astonishing diversity of the territory of the Tay, but it does so through the eyes of local people who speak for themselves about their lives by the river.

Nobody that I approached for an interview declined and all spoke of their appreciation of living in a beautiful part of the world. The river and its gifts are not taken for granted, and in these pages the people of the Tay speak for themselves about their concern to protect the environment and its wildlife.

I have tried to make this a 'tourist' book of a different type, in which the voice of local people is heard and something of the area's rich and colourful history is told. A number of appendices have been included to offer assistance to visitors seeking to sample the area's many attractions.

I am thankful to all of those who were interviewed for the book. Sadly, since he was interviewed, Fred Norrie (page 25) has died. A number of other individuals were also of great assistance. Bob Dakers and Gordon Douglas provided out-of-print books. Alan Richardson contributed photographs to supplement the work of Graham McGirk, as did the respective Museum Departments of Dundee and Perth district councils. Netta and Ben Gibson of Bendarroch House in Strathtay offered a refuge. Bill Slidders, Mark Stewart, Helen Brown, Neil Mudie and Jim Rougvie gave up their time to offer suggestions and proof-read the final manuscript. Bill Campbell of Mainstream Publishing also deserves thanks for his patience. Finally, I am endebted to my colleague at Dundee Press Agency, Lewis Thomson, who undertook many of the interviews and whose efforts made this book possible.

Chapter I

RESPECT THE RIVER

From the North Sea, on a summer's day, the yawning Tay estuary assumes an almost exotic quality. The sandy shores of Angus and Fife reach out on either side, a golden fringe on a fecund and mellow landscape of green, gold and now bright yellow on both sides of the river. Shimmering in the distance, the Tay's two mightiest bridges span the river's silver waters linking Dundee and the ancient Kingdom of Fife. Beyond them lie the mountains of Perthshire and the Scottish heartland.

It is a stirring spectacle which has evoked powerful and very different emotions down the centuries. For the whaler crews returning to what was Britain's principal whaling port it meant the end of months of isolation in the oceans of the Arctic and Antarctica. And it was a welcome sight to the seamen returning with their cargoes of coarse jute to the British Empire's 'Juteopolis' on the north banks of the Tay. But for the thousands who crammed aboard emigrant ships in the nineteenth century to escape grim poverty and disease it was a harsh and brutal land which spurned its own people.

Centuries before, the invading armies of the Danes and English viewed the sight with trepidation, fearing the fate which befell earlier would-be conquerors – an entire Roman legion lost in the glens of Perthshire and Angus never to be heard tell of again.

To invaders, the Tay was a dagger pointed straight at the heart of Scotland, a navigable artery to Perth, Scotland's ancient capital, and to the Highlands and lowland central belt. What made the river strategic then would later make it an important viaduct for trade.

On the southern shore Tentsmuir Point prods at the North Sea like an accusing finger defying the cold grey tide to break on its beaches. The thick pine forest, much of it planted in the 1920s, provides a dark-green backdrop to one of Scotland's most magnificent and least-known stretches of unspoilt sand dune.

Tentsmuir got its name after shipwrecked Danes erected makeshift shelters on what was then an exposed moor and is now almost completely afforested. Forestry trails maintained by country rangers cut through 14 square kilometres of forest allowing access to picnic areas and wildlife habitats. As country ranger Tony Wilson explains, 'Our main work is maintaining the rights of way in our area and making sure these are accessible to the public. During the summer months we take people on guided walks through forest tracks and explain our work and the forest wildlife.'

And there is no shortage of wildlife. The forest has a huge bat population; butterflies still abound in numbers rarely seen since the advent of pesticide spraying; thousands of eider duck, including the rare King Eider, converge each year on Tayport Bay; dolphins venture into the rivermouth; seals sun themselves on Abertay sands and harriers and peregrines hover over clearings and open ground.

The variety of flora and fauna reflects a remarkable mixture of habitats within a relatively small area. 'I enjoy working in this area enormously,' enthuses Tony. 'We are lucky to have a wide variety of landscapes. Moorland, rocky shoreline, sandy bays, pine and broadleafed forest and the large estuary mean that we have the potential for many more projects than we undertake today.

'Most of the countryside south of the Tay is intensively farmed and is under private ownership, so our work is determined by land use. We take birdwatching parties and guided walks to Tayport Bay and around the Newport area.

'To avoid problems with landowners, we stick to signposted tracks. One of the most popular is the Wormit to Balmerino right-of-way. It is just over two and a half miles long and goes through rough cattle pasture. The track overlooks the river and follows a steep embankment to finish at Balmerino Abbey. You can see the old salmon fishing stations along the coast and a wreck can be seen at low tide. The salmon stations were active until the 1950s and it was an important local industry. The fishermen went out in cobles built in a yard at Montrose. The old shacks are scattered all along the foreshore and the area is still popular with wildfowlers and anglers.'

Tony's colleague Ian Marshall welcomes the growing awareness of the need for conservation measures: 'The Forestry Commission is becoming much more aware of the need for conservation these days and has been mixing broadleafed trees with the ranks of conifers lately. And we have two nature conservancy council reserves at Tentsmuir and Morton lochs as well as a site of Special Scientific Interest at Flisk woods which is noted for its woodland fauna and big leafed trees,' he says.

For one local conservation enthusiast the Tay and 'green' issues have been a lifelong passion. Dr John Berry comes from one of Newport's oldest families and has lived at Tayfield House for most of his life since his birth in 1907. A pioneering conservationist, Dr Berry's commitment to the river and, above all, its geese has never faltered. While at Cambridge in the 1930s, he founded the Wildfowl Trust with the late Sir Peter Scott and went on to join the International Wildfowl Research Bureau. John's interest in conservation was sparked by his love of the geese which flock to the Tay each year. Like generations of Taysiders, as a boy each autumn he lifted his eyes in fascination to watch the skeins of pinkfooted geese arrive and herald the approach of winter.

Today the splendid grounds of Tayfield House still provide a refuge for the wild geese which John began to catch and breed as a boyhood hobby. The concern he shared with Peter Scott over threats to geese breeding grounds eventually led John to make one of the earliest scientific studies of Scottish geese and to the publication of his book *The Status of Wildfowl in Scotland*.

John delights in being called 'an old Goose-Berry' and recalls some of his achievements with pride. 'I was the first man to photograph a newly-hatched pinkfooted goose and I also found out which feathers the barnacle goose uses to line its nest – not their breast feathers as was thought but their underwing feathers. All of this information was gleaned here at Tayfield.'

Dr John 'Goose' Berry at Tayfield House

He is proud too, of his involvement in conservation and not just in the safeguarding of wildfowl. 'I was one of the people in the 1930s who warned about pollution and was seen as a bit of a crank. But I am sad to see that a lot of my prophecies are starting to come true. I am involved with the Tay River Purification Board and have helped them in the fight against pollution.'

In 1931 John lived on a boat on the Tay for nine weeks as part of a fishery research programme. He and his colleagues caught salmon in numbers which Tay anglers today could only dream of. He reports, 'We had special nets and could catch over 400 salmon in an hour for tagging. Later, with the Hydro-Board, I was involved in building fish passes to allow the salmon upstream to their spawning grounds.'

Contemplating a long and satisfying career, John echoes the sentiments of many when he talks about the river and countryside he loves: 'The Tay is a lovely area to live in and has been an inspiration for my life's work and achievements. It is a special area because it is so relatively unspoiled. The variety and numbers of birds, animals and fish that can be found is a gladdening sight. My life has been interesting and I could not wish for a better place than the Tay to help nurture my dreams and involve me so much.'

For the Berry family Newport has been home since 1788 when an earlier John Berry developed the Tayfield estate. The village is rather more douce than its neighbour to the east, the old ferry port of Tayport with its industrial heritage of shipbuilding and textiles. Many of

Kinshaldie Beach, Tentsmuir

Newport's solid Victorian merchant houses, which enjoy spectacular views across the river north to Dundee and the Sidlaws, began life as holiday homes for wealthy Dundee businessmen and textile magnates. Each summer they would send their families across the river and would commute by ferry. The children of the rich could enjoy the Fife countryside and, more importantly, escape overcrowded, squalid Dundee with its ever-present threat of disease during the hot summer months.

Originally named Seamills, Newport developed as one of four Fife ferry crossing points on the Tay estuary, the others being Tayport (then Ferryport-on-Craig), Woodhaven and Balmerino. The village developed rapidly with the growth of the ferry service — which, in 1715, is reputed to have helped Rob Roy MacGregor and his clansmen escape their pursuers. Until 1815 the ferry was a fairly disorganised affair but a tragedy that year, in which 15 passengers drowned, prompted the authorities to regulate the trade.

More prosperity came with the decision of Dundee's Guildry to open corn mills on the south bank of the river to supply the town's growing population. The link between Newport

Roger Kettle with 'Beau Peep'

13

and its larger northern neighbour was sealed, and when the first Tay Bridge was built it carried fresh water – just as the road bridge does today – from Dundee to its suburb in Fife.

Newport still has a well-to-do bourgeois feel about it, and residents have been able to take advantage of relatively low property prices for quality houses as many Dundonians have demonstrated a peculiar resistance to crossing the river to set up home. The village has been able to retain its identity and survive as a community despite the demise of its ferry service to Dundee and the eclipse of its once busy harbour. It has even withstood the arrival of artists and writers in such numbers that it merits the description, only slightly tongue-in-cheek, of being Dundee's 'Left Bank'. The wealth of creative talent in the Newport area comes as a surprise to smug outsiders who view Dundee and its suburbs as a cultural backwater. Residents include artist and playwright John Byrne, film-maker Tim Neat, acclaimed poet Douglas Dunn, painter Will Maclean, photographer Joseph Macleod, and writer and broadcaster Billy Kay.

They are all neighbours of another creative talent less well-known on the Scottish scene but whose work provides a daily fix of humour to millions across the world. Roger Kettle is the unassuming ideas man in a cartoon partnership with Andrew Christine which has produced no fewer than three cartoon strips that are syndicated across the world. The adventures of Foreign Legion anti-hero Beau Peep, who appears in the *Daily Star*, have captured the imagination of readers across five continents – including Foreign Legionnaires!

Thirteen annual 'Beau Peep' collections have sold an average of 50,000 copies and the exploits of 'A Man Called Horace' (*Daily Record/Daily Mirror*) and 'Mildew' (*News of the World*) now reach audiences in India and the United States. Beau Peep has joined Desperate Dan, Dennis the Menace, Oor Wullie, Mary Shelley's Frankenstein and Beatrix Potter's Peter Rabbit as a famous fictional character conceived on the banks of the Tay.

Roger, a member of the local pool team and an avid Dundee United fan, takes it all in his stride: 'I originally come from the Highlands and arrived in Dundee for an interview with the publishers D. C. Thomson. I wanted to be a journalist. I thought the interview was going really well until the guy said that I would be ideal for comics. I had never even thought of it before, but within weeks I was working on "Beryl the Peril" in the *Topper*.'

In 1977, on the strength of a couple of cartoons sold to a 'men's magazine', Roger took the audacious step of going freelance and spent the next 20 anxious months trying to sell 'Beau Peep' to the nation's newspapers.

'Now that we are successful, people in London constantly ask me why I don't move down there,' he says, 'But I love it here. Before my children arrived, the room I used as a study had a fantastic view over the Tay. As I worked I could sit and watch seals playing in the water. And here we are living in a self-contained village only five minutes from the city centre of Dundee. As a lifestyle, I think it is hard to beat.'

Just along the road from the Kettle household, Billy Kay has set up residence with his expanding family. Author of *Scots the Mither Tongue*, *Knee Deep in Claret* and editor of *The Dundee Book*, Billy first became known to Scottish audiences through his oral history *Odyssey* series for BBC Scotland. Chat shows in the Scots dialect followed and he has produced television programmes on the Scottish mining industry and on his adopted city across the water, Dundee.

Billy's discovery of and subsequent enchantment with the estuary and its countryside has a familiar ring to it. His visits to Dundee on business led to an interest first in Dundee United Football Club and then in Dundee's history. His hugely successful play, *They Fairly Mak Ye*

Broughty Ferry Castle – now a museum

Swans at Broughty Ferry

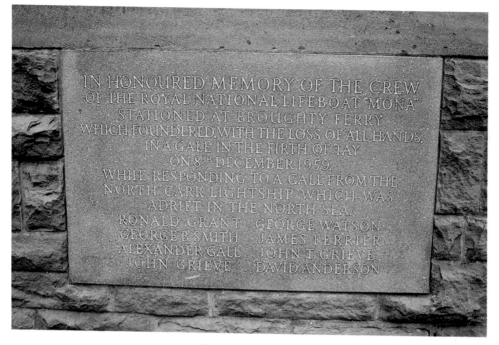

IN HONOURED MEMORY OF THE CREW
OF THE ROYAL NATIONAL LIFEBOAT 'MONA'
STATIONED AT BROUGHTY FERRY
WHICH FOUNDERED WITH THE LOSS OF ALL HANDS
IN A GALE IN THE FIRTH OF TAY
ON 8TH DECEMBER 1959
WHILE RESPONDING TO A CALL FROM THE
NORTH CARR LIGHTSHIP WHICH WAS
ADRIFT IN THE NORTH SEA
RONALD GRANT   GEORGE WATSON
GEORGE B SMITH   JAMES FERRIER
ALEXANDER GALL   JOHN T GRIEVE
JOHN GRIEVE   DAVID ANDERSON

The Mona *remembered*

Work, attracted record audiences to Dundee Rep. Before long Billy was hooked on the 'Tay lifestyle', almost a phenomenon in its own right.

In the comfort of his substantial Victorian villa overlooking the Tay he waxes lyrical, with the enthusiasm of a recent convert, about the surroundings he has made home. 'There is something about the river. Ever since I started coming through from Edinburgh to Dundee I have been fascinated by it and always felt at home when I crossed the river at Perth to travel alongside it.

'Now, living in Newport, we have a great view of the estuary. Seeing it gives me a lift, it has a great expansiveness – especially for me when I spend a lot of time at home working alone on a word processor. It really helps to put things into perspective.'

Across the river, Newport has its mirror image in Broughty Ferry, a reluctant suburb of Dundee whose inhabitants have a reputation of regarding 'the Ferry' as something special and themselves likewise. But in the last century West Ferry really was something special. As the favoured domicile of Dundee's textile magnates, the 'Jute Barons', the area acquired a not altogether unjustified reputation as 'the richest square mile in the British Empire'.

Today Broughty Ferry Castle keeps a silent vigil over the estuary, its cannons long silenced and its bloody, if ineffective, military history a distant memory captured in the castle's museum. Along the shore to the west of the castle the pebble beach is no longer host to the fisherfolk who hauled up their boats and dried their nets on the shoreline. The ferries have long ceased sailing from the tiny harbour. Its busiest role now is as a starting point for the annual August raft race and a New Year's Day 'dook' in the river. For the rest of the year, schoolboy anglers and older enthusiasts have the deserted pier to themselves.

Spirit of Tayside

The crew on exercise

A Victorian coxswain on the Tay

'The Ferry' may have become a desirable and populous suburb of Dundee, but it has fought tenaciously to keep its own individuality. Recent house-building is sympathetic to the fishing village heritage. And its quality shopping, pubs, cafés and restaurants make it a popular spot to while away an afternoon. Broughty Ferry beach, once an annual holiday mecca for thousands of Dundonians, may have declined in popularity but the first blink of summer sun still draws families to the waterside.

For all of its gentrification, Broughty Ferry cherishes its maritime connections. Those in search of the area's whaling and seafaring traditions can visit the Castle museum which houses a variety of displays, and snug rows of fishermen's cottages along the shore have stood the test of time – and weather. Some of the pubs, notably The Ship and The Fisherman's Tavern, have an authentic nautical atmosphere with, in the case of the former, spectacular views across the river to the harbour at Tayport (home to a thriving yachting fraternity).

Fishing at Broughty Ferry may have died out but a stern reminder of just how much of a working river the Tay remains is found in the Broughty Ferry Lifeboat Station. The lifeboat shed and the *Spirit of Tayside* moored offshore bear witness to the tenacity and courage of those who go to sea.

On a stormy night in December 1959, the Broughty Ferry lifeboat *Mona* was capsized and her crew of eight lost as she braved a storm to rescue the crew of the drifting North Carr Lightship. When daylight dawned the *Mona* was found beached on Buddon Sands with five of her volunteers drowned in the vessel's wheelhouse. It was the end of 24 years' service for a vessel which had been launched on 72 occasions and saved 118 lives.

The loss of the *Mona* and her crew stunned the local community and shocked the nation. And when the local RNLI called for volunteers to form a new crew they were greeted with 36 applications and the station was once again operational. To this day, donations to the RNLI from Tayside are among the highest in the country.

Hugh Scott, deputy coxswain of the *Spirit of Tayside*, has been involved with the lifeboat for 20 years: 'The lifeboat crew has a pool of 20 men and we also have a small inshore rescue boat,' he explains. 'The average number of calls we receive is around one every two months for the big boat and once or twice a month for the small, inshore boat. As a lifeboat, we do not get involved in the politics of safety – we leave that to the coastguard. We are just there to act.'

And Hugh, who appropriately enough works as general manager of the RRS *Discovery*, is a keen Tay sailor: 'I was brought up sailing and was at sea for nine years. I live beside and overlook the Tay and it's something I cannot get away from. Like many people involved in the lifeboat I am a keen member of the Royal Tay Yacht Club and while the Tay is in many ways a restricting river for the serious sailor, it is a great river nonetheless. The vagaries of tide and weather mean that if you have learned the craft of seamanship on the Tay, you have had a very good training indeed.'

In the Middle Ages the Tay became an important Scottish window for trade with the Baltic and the rest of Europe. The marine traffic of the 1990s is much diminished but remains important; shipping is once again on the increase, with prosperity gracing the ports of Perth and Dundee.

But the shifting sands and treacherous waters of the Tay have taken their toll over the centuries and it is estimated that, since Roman times, up to five thousand vessels may have foundered in the estuary. Among the wrecks which litter the river-bed are General Monck's booty-laden treasure ships which sank in a storm after the sacking of Dundee in 1651. In the nineteeth century the loss of Baltic traders, schooners and brigs was quite common. Nowadays ships in distress are a rarity thanks largely to modern navigational aids and the indispensable local knowledge of the Tay's hardy band of river pilots.

One man who knows more than most about the estuary is Allan Ramsay, who has lived all of his life by the river and spent 23 years working for the University of Dundee's Tay Estuary Research Centre at Newport. Allan rates himself lucky to have been able to indulge his passion for the river and earn a living at the same time. He expands on the story of Monck's treasure: 'It is believed that when General Monck sacked Dundee and destroyed the port, he put millions of pounds' worth of treasure on small ships and despatched them southwards. There are no records of these ships ever reaching their destination so it is presumed that the treasure must lie somewhere in the Abertay sands.'

The lure of Monck's lost booty has inspired its share of treasure-seekers. Salvage companies have employed modern technology in the hunt, and promising blips have appeared on the screens of their sub-bottom profilers, magnatometers and sidescans. So far, however, the river has refused to yield a hoard which could be worth tens of millions of pounds – and the mystery of Monck's treasure endures.

Now in his 60s, Allan has seen plenty of changes on the river: 'I first started sailing on the river as a boy of nine out of Newport and the differences over the years are immense. Although still one of Britain's cleanest rivers because of the huge volume of water it carries, there is much more pollution apparent than 40 years ago. Oil is the main culprit. I was secretary of the Royal Tay Yacht Club in the 1950s when it was rare for a boat to be affected by oil – but now it is so bad it isn't even worth cleaning the oil off boats. There has always been dumping in the river but it is only recent industrial dumping that has made such a difference.

'I have a real love of working on the river and an interest in boats has been paramount all through my life,' says Allan, a proud inhabitant of Newport who gave up his job as an accountant to work on the Tay. 'Until the 1960s many people kept small boats in the Earl Grey dock in Dundee and, with the ferries and the shipyards, there was a real community feel about the river. These small boats were not of good quality and this group disappeared with the advent of the road bridge. There was also a collapse in the rowing clubs which once thrived on the river. The Corinthians and the Broughty Ferry clubs used to hold keen competitions, but sailing gradually took over, and yachting – once a rich man's sport – has become more accessible.'

Dozens of yachts moored at Broughty Ferry, Newport and Tayport bear witness to the popularity of sailing in the estuary. The Royal Tay Yacht Club celebrated its centenary in 1985 and the club has grown from humble beginnings to occupy a splendidly refurbished clubhouse with a membership of around seven hundred and a full racing programme for dinghies, catamarans and keelboats.

'There has been a tremendous boom in sailing over the last decade,' reports lifeboatman Hugh Scott. 'Club yachting on the Tay is well organised and self-sufficient. It is usually the individual sailor who gets into trouble. The majority of people using the river treat it with the utmost respect due to the erratic nature of its tides and sandbanks.'

Allan Ramsay has seen the hazards of the rivermouth at first hand. 'There are plenty of wrecks around the estuary. In one storm at the turn of the century 20 ships were wrecked out there in two days. They are still there. The sand builds up and washes around them. I have seen the sternpost of a ship in the pool near Abertay. The Abertay sands are very dangerous for small boats. They are constantly shifting and the resulting shallowness means that often there is only a few inches of water below the keel of the boat.

'The Tay is a difficult area to navigate as vessels out at sea cannot see the channel entrance as they approach the estuary. It must have been a nightmare before the electric age. The hill at Munzien by Cupar was known as the "Visible Hill" and was used as a navigation device, but visibility would still have played its part. The channel is less than a half a mile wide at the estuary entrance. A few years ago the cruise ship *Uganda* ran aground on a sandbank.'

For 24 years Ron Hogg, as one of the Tay's river pilots, has been charged with avoiding such calamities and has learned of the idiosyncracies and dangers that lurk in an estuary where the tide can race to seven knots. He has seen his share of drama too on the 'high seas' of the Tay: 'The main problem for ships coming into the estuary is the notorious Tay Bar. It is an enormous sandbank that all the charts warn about. The North Sea is very deep, but when you get to Barry, there is a massive shallowing. It's the equivalent of hitting a cliff when you walk along a narrow street.

'South-east gales in the North Sea build up enormous swells which rush into the estuary. When these huge swells hit the sand, they shoot up into the air. Often there are build-ups of

Tayport harbour

two or three at a time. Few people have seen them, but those of us who have, know that the Tay can be vicious. A regular tale is of the monster swell which takes ships by surprise. These things are the multistoreys of waves. Ships come in to Dundee with their hulls buckled by waves. People don't believe the strength and power that the water has.'

Those who underestimate the river do so at their peril and on one occasion a ship's captain's foolhardiness resulted in an unscheduled trip to Holland for Ron: 'Once I went out to guide out a tanker from Dundee in high water when the swells were at their worst. I said to the captain that he had better batten down the hatches. He just laughed and replied that his ship had been through typhoons and that a piddling little Scottish river wouldn't bother him. I warned him that there was no room for manoeuvre and that once you go, you have to keep going. We set off and things were really wild. This tanker was about five storeys high and the waves were curling right over us. There was no way I could get off the ship and return so I ended up in Rotterdam!

'The Tay is really changeable weatherwise. The wind speed is affected by the hills and can whip up the water into a ferocious storm. Even within half an hour, the wind can get up from Force 3 to Force 12. Ships have to be "sat in" or there is a real danger that some of them could flip over.'

The seven pilots who work the river are self-employed and 'live' their job with call-outs day and night. The trusted guides to treacherous local waters, they are no strangers to danger. In the last 20 years, one pilot has died and another lost a foot after becoming trapped between two ships. But for all the hazards, Ron relishes his work and, like so many who work on the river, loves the Tay. 'Piloting is a very enjoyable job. You never know what the day will bring. It is exciting and can get the adrenaline going – personal judgment is crucial in all aspects of the job. The Tay is a beautiful area to work in. The sights that I see at six in the morning coming down to Dundee are amazing. The whole river is lit up. Once, when the cruise ship SS *Uganda* came in, the captain woke up all the passengers to let them see the beauty of the Tay. He said that it was a spectacle unrivalled in all his years at sea.'

Among those who had more time than most – and more than they would have wished – to appreciate the spectacle of the Tay estuary were the boy trainees aboard the Training Ship *Mars*, one of the most unusual vessels to feature in the river's maritime history.

The *Mars* was moored for 60 years in the river just off Woodhaven in Fife, and for long after the mere mention of its name was enough to produce compliance in the most rebellious of Dundonian offspring. The threat of being sent to Mars was well understood to be an all too terrestrial experience.

The *Mars* arrived in the Tay in 1869 following a public petition which demanded the establishment of an industrial school for 'friendless and destitute boys'. None of the 6,560 'bad boys' who underwent training for a career in the Royal Navy or merchant fleet was guilty of any crime. Truancy and constant trouble-making was enough to merit a spell aboard the feared training ship.

Conditions for the four hundred boys aged 12 to 16 were, to say the least, harsh. Reveille at 6 a.m. was followed by a cold shower pumped straight from the river in summer and winter. The boys were referred to by their number rather than name and the staff were quick to resort to the tawse. Not surprisingly, there were riots and mutinies by the inmates who were often underfed, and on one occasion the captain's quarters were set on fire. Attempted escapes were rare and hazardous – one attempt in 1871 ended in three boys drowning. Their grave can still be seen in nearby Forgan cemetery. In 1879 the *Mars* played a brief role in the Tay's best-known drama, when the vessel made an unsuccessful attempt to rescue victims of the Tay Bridge Disaster.

Today, the remaining piers of that doomed structure poke out of the swirling waters of the estuary to keep pace with its successor. A grim monument to man's fallibility before the forces of nature, the columns are an unnerving reminder to present-day rail travellers of the tragedy which befell their predecessors on a dark and stormy winter's evening.

Formally opened on 1 June 1878, the bridge was a miracle of modern engineering. At almost two miles long, the single-track bridge which spanned the Tay estuary was by far the longest in the world. The following year, in June 1879, Queen Victoria crossed the bridge on her return journey from Balmoral, and later knighted Thomas Bouch, the 58-year-old designer of the greatest iron structure the world had ever seen. With the British Empire at its zenith and Dundee's textile barons at the peak of their fabulous wealth, the bridge was a fitting symbol of British omnipotence.

The jute merchants and flax-spinners of Dundee along with the directors of the North British Railway raised the fantastic sum of £300,000 to fund a project which, in the six years of its construction, consumed 10,000,000 bricks, 4,000 tons of cast iron, 15,000 casks of cement — and the lives of 20 of the workmen who risked life and limb daily to accomplish an outstanding feat of Victorian engineering.

The achievement inspired William Topaz McGonagall, the self-styled 'poet and tragedian' to new poetic heights. But, prophetically, McGonagall, not normally noted for his caution and reserve, chose to hedge his bets! He wrote:

Salvage operations after the Tay Bridge disaster of 1879

> Beautiful Railway Bridge of the Silvery Tay!
> And prosperity to Provost Cox, who has given
> Thirty thousand pounds and upwards away
> In helping to erect the Bridge of the Tay,
> Most handsome to be seen,
> Near by Dundee and the Magdalen Green.

He reflected local scepticism when he added:

> Beautiful Railway Bridge of the Silvery Tay!
> I hope that God will protect all passengers
> By night and by day,
> And that no accident will befall them while crossing
> The Bridge of the Silvery Tay,
> For that moment would be most awful to be seen
> Near by Dundee and the Magdalen Green.

Before the year's end the bridge was to claim 75 more lives when, on 28 December, the evening train from Edinburgh to Dundee crept on to the bridge during a howling gale with winds raging at 70 miles per hour and more. As the train moved across Bouch's impressive high girders the bridge collapsed, taking the engine, its six carriages and passengers with it. There was no chance of survival in the icy waters of the estuary and for months afterwards bodies were washed up along the river.

The bridge lay shattered, and with it the career of Sir Thomas Bouch who never recovered from the trauma and died a broken man. The ubiquitous McGonagall was on hand to pen an epitaph:

> Beautiful Railway Bridge of the Silvery Tay!
> Alas! I am very sorry to say
> That ninety lives have been taken away
> On the last Sabbath day of 1879
> Which will be remembered for a very long time.

One of the members of the subsequent Court of Inquiry found that the bridge had been 'badly designed, badly constructed and badly maintained'.

Undeterred by the devastating events which had brought the press to Dundee from around the world, the local business community demonstrated admirable perseverance when it raised backing for a replacement bridge. Despite the disturbing thrift of including 118 girders from the collapsed bridge, the new structure cost £670,000, double the price of its predecessor. Work began in 1882 and the bridge was opened to traffic on 20 June 1887. Thirteen men died in its construction but their work has stood the test of time: in 1987 an estimated quarter of a million people turned out to witness a spectacular fireworks display to celebrate its centenary. The bridge still carries traffic today, albeit with speed restrictions and the precaution of allowing only one train at a time across the high girders.

For almost 25 years Peter McPherson has worked on the bridge, supervising the year-round maintenance programme that the bridge has in common with its better-known cousin spanning the Forth. It is a job which has become a way of life: 'The bridge is a great location to work in. There is plenty of good fresh air, although it can get really cold, and you can see four seasons in one day. We can see the rain coming in and tell when bad weather is due. There is a real sense of knowing nature by looking at the sky and at the river.'

The allure of working on the bridge extends to most of the 21 platers, welders, painters and joiners who work on the bridge. Once acclimatised, staff tend to stay with the bridge for many years in a tight fraternity, bound together by their unusual, unending task. Peter is proud that, unlike the neighbouring road bridge, his charge has never had to close due to bad weather, allowing 88 trains to cross the estuary every day. Problems with massive ice floes have eased with recent climatic changes and the bridge does not suffer much from salt water corrosion. Most damage to piers is caused by the tides and is repaired within strict safety parameters that have ensured that there have been no fatalities since 1967.

One of the biggest headaches for the maintenance men comes from a surprising source: 'We have a major problem on the bridge with starlings,' says Peter. It is no joke. He goes on, 'Over *one million pairs* roost on the bridge. These and the seagulls are the major causes of fouling on the bridge and all this muck has to be scraped off, which is not a pleasant task. We section off the areas that are being worked on but it would be crazy to try and get rid of the birds. We have no culls – they would just continue to come anyway. For the guys working on the booms a nice seagull egg is a treat for breakfast. But a large slice of our budget goes on dealing with this fouling problem.'

Extensive use of the girders from the ill-fated first bridge has been made in its successor. The majority of the outside girders are from the old bridge – only 16 of the original girders were not recycled. And the bridge still attracts considerable attention.

'We get a lot of enquiries from people interested in the bridge,' reports Peter. 'Tours are organised mainly for civil engineering students and railway buffs interested in the types of steel and methods of construction used.'

The opening of the railway bridge did much to diminish business for the old ferries which plied between Fife and the harbours of Broughty Ferry and Dundee. In turn, it was expected that the opening of the road bridge in 1966 would produce a downturn in rail bridge traffic. In recent years, however, with congested roads and parking difficulties, the reverse has been the case and the number of trains crossing the Tay is on the increase.

Commuters to Dundee from Fife have mounted a voluble and convincing campaign to re-establish a halt at Wormit and have won the tentative support of local authorities. So far, ScotRail has refused to acknowledge local demand and this, along with looming privatisation and the excessive costs of maintaining both the Forth and Tay Bridges, must cast a shadow over the future of a structure which has stood for over a century.

Nonetheless, cynics speculate as to whether the Tay Road Bridge will outlast its senior neighbour. Built 80 years later, the road bridge is subject to almost permanent maintenance work tackling costly corrosion and design flaws. But, with over 20,000 vehicles a day using the bridge, none can deny the benefits it has brought. At 2.2 kilometres long, it is Britain's longest river crossing. The tolls are used for bridge upkeep and to service the original loan of £6.7 million borrowed to build the bridge – the current debt stands at £6.9 million!

The bridge employs a team of 38 men. Most are toll-collectors and life can be more interesting than it might at first appear. Harry Byers and Jim Macdonald stress that the job has its ups and downs: 'The public are quite cheery and we do have a laugh with them. Money is

An early ferry leaves Broughty Ferry

sometimes a problem. People hand over £50 notes expecting change on a 40p crossing and the odd tourist tries to pay by cheque.

'But on patrols there are often problems with suicides and that is a sad and messy job.' Yet black humour on the bridge wins through: 'One night a patrolman found a bike abandoned and assumed that a suicide had taken place. He reported it and gave the bike to the police. But the next day the bloke turned up looking for his bike: he had been too drunk to cycle so gave up and walked home.'

'The odd drunk tries to throw himself off the bridge shouting, "Tell her I love her!" and we have to drag them to safety. Guys do stupid things when they've had a few, and some throw themselves off at low tide and we have to unstick them from the mud.' But with the real thing, the mess and heartbreak are awful.

'In the winter it is always freezing and there are problems with fog, ice and wind. Accidents are easily caused in this sort of weather and it's difficult to explain to people that they should ca' canny when they are in a hurry. People have overturned their cars on foggy days and hit the central reservation. They usually claim they were only doing five miles an hour but you only have to look at the state of their cars to know the full story.'

As the last road bridge employee to have worked on the 'Fifie' ferries, Fred Norrie is well placed to put the bridge into perspective. He joined the 'Fifies' in 1942 and remained a crew member until 1966 when the ferry service made way for the new bridge. Despite his long years of service, Fred has few illusions about the ferries which are so fondly remembered by Dundonians and Fifers alike: 'By 1966 the ferries were swamped with people and they could not cope. The bridge was really vital in getting more people across the river in less time. The big disadvantage of the ferries was that they were so slow and were always off in fog and high winds. The timetable always emphasised "weather permitting". It wasn't a very reliable service.

'About 45 of us were employed on the ferries – most were ex-merchant navy and they called the ferries a "shore job". In those days we had full employment so the end of the ferries was not a great strain and most of the staff moved to the bridge when it opened. We did miss the lack of contact with the public. The ferries might not be able to cope with the pressures of today, but they had a charm and romance all of their own. They provided people with a link to the river which a road bridge just does not do. I have pleasant memories of helping with "stay-at-home" holidays during the war when we ran trips for Dundee families up the river to Newburgh. The last ever ferry trip was on 18 August 1966. It was an evening fund-raising event for the Royal National Lifeboat Institution and there was a service on Newport pier.

'The river has been part of my life and I am grateful to have worked on it. There's nothing to compare with it for fresh air and some stunning views. But it is changed days and I regret the decline of the docks and the end of shipbuilding on the Tay.'

It is difficult today to believe that the Tay was once second only to the Clyde as a Scottish shipbuilding centre. Shipbuilding in Dundee was strangled in 1980 when British Shipbuilders succeeded in closing the Robb Caledon yard after a lengthy occupation by the workforce. It marked the end of an era. Thousands of Dundonians served their apprenticeships in 'the yard' over the years, often learning as much about trade unionism and socialism as shipbuilding.

Oil-rig fabrication took over from shipbuilding at the waterfront, but few Dundonians are aware that the city has retained an important link with shipbuilding. Marine Design Consultants Ltd keeps the 200-year-old shipbuilding tradition alive by producing designs for orders all over the world. Technical officer Alistair Tosh began his working life as a trainee in 1950 in the technical office of Robb Caledon, the Tay's last yard. He regrets the demise of shipbuilding on the Tay and puts a passionate and cogent argument for why it should never have been allowed to happen: 'The Tay was, and still is, well suited for shipbuilding. It has deep water and there were no restrictions on launching – it is much more suitable than the Clyde which has major problems with available space on land and problems in launching. In many ways, the Dundee yard was an ideal site. There was plenty of space for fitting out and a lot of room for equipment on the ground.

'Maybe if the Caledon had not been nationalised in 1977, things might have been different. But Dundee was one of the yards lined up for the chop to comply with the European edict on reducing shipbuilding capacity.'

His colleague Bill Bennet agrees and he voices the frustration of many that the Tay estuary, recently a harbour to giant oil platforms and a limited offshore traffic, has never benefited to any significant extent from Scotland's oil boom: 'The closure of the shipyard was one which we are very unhappy with. It was a political rather than a purely economic decision. The loss of the shipyard meant that Dundee lost its traditional shipbuilding unit and the skills and jobs which went with it. There was a knock-on effect too for the harbour which had benefited enormously from the shipyard with its use of the dry-dock and the incoming timber and steel.

'The Caledon was never part of any major investment programme that may have saved the works. If a bigger dry dock had been built, and covered berths constructed, Dundee with the big Tay estuary would have been ideal for the oil industry, closer to the oilfields and better suited than Aberdeen.'

Marine Design Consultants has diversified into the offshore oil industry, civil engineering and computer services. But the company still produces designs, production drawings and costings for yards all over Britain as well as countries as disparate as Indonesia, Russia and Dubai.

MDC may be forward-looking but, after 40 years working at the harbour, Alistair Tosh allows himself the luxury of looking back. 'All my working life has been spent by the river. I enjoy the work and have always been involved in shipbuilding and shipping. If a guy enters a shipyard as an apprentice there is a good chance he will want to spend his whole working life in that industry. There is something very appealing about working by the water. I miss the bustle of the harbour as it was when I started, and it is a shame that there is no fishing any more out of Dundee. It was quite a sight to see the fishing boats and the tugs and the lines of ships waiting for berths. But there is still a lot going on here with grain, paper and the new North Sea survival school.'

Shipbuilding was thriving in Dundee as long ago as 1792 when Robert Small wrote: 'Shipbuilding is supposed to be executed here with great advantage and ingenuity. In it two masters are employed, with 31 journeymen and apprentices, and six are employed by two persons who build boats.' The trade grew and in 1824 striking shipyard workers in Dundee entered labour history when they resolved to 'manufacture for themselves' and set up their own yard, almost 150 years before the famous work-in at Upper Clyde Shipbuilders.

The lasting monument to the bygone skills of Dundee's shipyard workers is the Royal Research Ship *Discovery* which has become an inspiring symbol of the new Dundee. The vessel's triumphant return to the Tay in 1986, where it was first launched in 1901, brought thousands out to line the banks of the river and witness an historic homecoming.

Much of the public interest arises, of course, from the vessel's association with Captain Robert Falcon Scott and the National Antarctic Expedition he led between 1901 and 1904. *Discovery* was specially built for the voyage by Dundee Shipbuilders at a cost of £51,000, and was the first British ship to be specifically designed for scientific exploration.

During the expedition, the ship became trapped in pack ice for two years, when her strengthened beams and hull were put to the ultimate test by the enormous pressures of the ice. Eventually, two other Dundee ships, the *Terra Nova* and the *Morning* came to her rescue and the *Discovery* was blasted free. It was the *Terra Nova* and not, as is often imagined, the *Discovery* that later took Captain Scott on his ill-fated expedition of 1910.

Scott's exploits are commemorated in displays and exhibitions on the *Discovery*, finally berthed a few hundred yards from where it first entered the water. The ship is at the centre of a unique heritage centre constructed as part of Dundee's controversial Waterfront Development.

The ship's return captured the imagination of Dundonians and the vessel became identified with a resurgence of self-confidence in its home town. RRS *Discovery* is now one of Dundee's best-known tourist attractions. Hugh Scott, the ship's general manager, reports: 'The arrival of *Discovery* in Dundee and its role as a tourist attraction has definitely given a maritime awareness to the area. Last year we had 50,000 visitors to the ship and we get a lot of children and school parties. The teacher who guides the groups around the ship is an ex-seaman and he shows the kids aspects of seamanship from navigation to the charts and equipment.'

The *Discovery* is still undergoing restoration which will take several years to complete, and

Hugh Scott, Ship's Master, RRS Discovery

shipwrights from Arbroath, where until recently wooden fishing boats were constructed, have been recruited for their specialised skills. Resplendent in her new rigging and gleaming brass and paintwork, RRS *Discovery* is an impressive sight. But it takes an inspection of the vessel in the company of its former ship's master Bill MacGregor for the landlubber to appreciate *Discovery*'s secrets and her masterly craftsmanship.

A time-served shipwright from Aberdour in Fife, Bill is a keen member of the World Ships Society and his painstaking detective work unearthed new details of the vessel's construction: 'We have identified 25 different woods used in her construction,' he says. 'Some of them are rare and expensive to buy nowadays and at least one, the Moulmain teak from Thailand used for the decks, is no longer available and its nearest equivalent costs an astonishing £2,000 per cubic metre.'

Bill adds that the hull is made up of three layers of wood around double frames and it is never less than 26 inches deep. Pitch pine and English elm form the outer layer; 6-inch-thick Greenheart from Guyana, the second-hardest wood in the world, is the second layer; and a lining of pitch pine, originally Riga fir, makes up the inner hull. The closely spaced frames are

Discovery *at Cowes, 1901*

made of Scottish oak, and Bill has traced its origins to Perthshire, the Borders and Renfrewshire.

It was this feat of marine engineering, coupled with a bow of 11ft-thick solid oak, plated with steel, which assured the ship's survival during her two years as a prisoner of the pack ice. But the quality of the workmanship does little to help its modern custodians. 'The irony is that the ship is so well built and crafted that any repair is extremely difficult,' explains Bill. 'Each plank has had to be individually steamed into place. She was launched in 1901 with a 20-year life-span and therefore not built for repair, but so far we have overcome any hurdles.'

There were several other novel features to the vessel. To preserve the timber, hollows in the frames were packed with rock salt. It was, however, a safety device which almost sank the ship: 'In 1979 the Royal Navy mistook the remnants of the salt for signs of rot and decided to tow her out to the Atlantic for missile practice. It was only the timely intervention of the Maritime Trust that saved her.'

Like the adventurers of today, Scott and his colleagues sought commercial sponsorship. Six compass manufacturers sent their compasses for testing near the South Pole, adding a further twist to the ship's specifications. A 30ft-wide zone of the vessel is completely free of ferrous metal. 'All fittings are brass or bronze,' explains Bill, 'and even the buttons on the mattresses were made of wood. The crew had no metal fittings on their clothing right down to the eyelets on their shoes, which had to be made of leather.'

Berthed nearby *Discovery* is Dundee's second historic ship, HMS *Unicorn*. Built in Chatham as one of a class of four 46-gun frigates, the *Unicorn* arrived in Dundee long before *Discovery* was even built. She has been part of the scenery at Dundee harbour since 1873 and is the oldest ship of the line still afloat.

Rennie Stewart, captain of the vessel, was involved in the appeal to save the *Unicorn* from the breaker's yard and is an authority on her history. He reveals that the ship was in naval use until surprisingly recently: 'The *Unicorn* was headquarters of the senior naval officer for the Tay during both World Wars. It was also headquarters of the Royal Navy Voluntary Reserve East Coast of Scotland Section. The RNVR was formed at the turn of the century to train civilians in aspects of the senior service. Between the wars the *Unicorn* division was famed for its prowess in boxing, and matches were held on board which attracted up to four hundred spectators. At the outbreak of the Second World War, two Polish submarines arrived in the Tay after a daring escape from the advancing Germans at Gdansk. The heroism of the crews was recognised later in the war when the Polish Commander-in-Chief, General Sikorsky, decorated them aboard the *Unicorn*.'

After the war, the *Unicorn* resumed its role as a base for the Royal Navy Reserve but in the 1960s a shore base, HMS Camperdown, was opened and the RNR no longer had any real use for the ship. The new onshore headquarters remains the base for the Tay's active RNR detachment of 100 officers and 160 ratings along with a 40-strong Royal Marines Reserve and a popular sea cadet unit.

As it slipped further into disrepair, the total demise of the *Unicorn* seemed inevitable, but in 1967 a society headed by the Earl of Dalhousie was established to preserve the vessel. Two thousand pounds was quickly raised but the real breakthrough came after a surprising personal connection prompted a large donation. As Rennie recalls, 'The *Unicorn*'s future was secured when John Smith, a leading figure in Coutt's Bank in London, read about our appeal in the *Daily Telegraph*. During the war he had flown flying-boats which were based on the Tay at Woodhaven and met his wife in Dundee. She was a Wren serving on the *Unicorn* and this personal connection led him to persuade the Manifold Trust to make a £5,000 donation. Since then the *Unicorn* has become a floating museum and is the oldest British-built warship still afloat.'

The *Unicorn* and the *Discovery* are now among the few ships which have Dundee as a home port – a far cry from the middle of the nineteenth century when almost three hundred vessels – whalers, coasters, jute traders, clippers, fishing boats and ferries – were registered at the port. Dundee largely owes its existence to the port, which for a crucial period of the city's history between 1764 and 1815, was virtually the only source of revenue for the Town Council. The sheltered harbour made sense of Dundee's location and was the scene of early human settlement.

One of the earliest references to Dundee's port records the arrival in 1040 of the Scottish king Malcolm Canmore and his troops in hot pursuit of the errant Macbeth. Gradually trade with the Baltic and Flanders developed to become a staple of the harbour for more than five centuries. In the thirteenth century wine was imported into Dundee, and by 1620 the city had grown to become Scotland's second largest importer of wine, landing 50,000 gallons from France and Spain. There were other exotic imports too: shipping lists from around this period mention 'murmblade' (marmalade from Spain – exploding the myth of Mrs Keiller inventing the preserve in her Dundee kitchen), Canary sugar, aniseed oil, 'toffie' from Flanders and 'oly-doly' (olive oil) from Spain. These luxurious imports are a further indication that although Dundee may have only been Scotland's third city in terms of population, it was higher up the league table of wealth and influence.

In turn, the port exported wool, sheepskins and hides until the fifteenth century when the arrival of Flemish weavers in the East of Scotland brought the new industries of spinning,

Dundee harbour in the sixteenth century

weaving and cloth manufacture. For the next three hundred years textiles would dominate trade at the harbour.

The modern port developed after 1815 with extensive works by the noted engineer, Thomas Telford, and continued with the creation of the Dundee Harbour Trust in 1830. The establishment of the new Harbour Board coincided with the rise of the jute industry and the expansion of shipbuilding which produced a rapid growth in facilities in the middle of the 1800s.

Recent years have witnessed substantial investment in the port by Dundee Port Authority, an encouraging vote of confidence in the harbour's future. Between 1986 and 1991, £9 million was spent to make the port one of the most modern in Scotland. New deep-water berths and wharves have been created to meet the needs of the offshore oil industry, a roll-on roll-off terminal, new storage facilities, modern cranes and high-security lorry parking have all been added to the harbour's amenities.

The panelled splendour of Captain John Watson's surroundings in his spacious office at the Harbour Chambers speak volumes for the prosperity which graced the port of Dundee in bygone years. But, as chief executive of Dundee Port Authority, he is confident about the future: 'The fortunes of Dundee's port have changed over the years. But we are a success for our size. In 1989 we had a turnover of £4.5 million and a pre-tax profit of £1.2 million, which represented an increase of £400,000 over the previous year. Of course, the decline of jute has had an impact. In 1933, some 233,000 tonnes of raw jute was landed here; today the figure is about 11,000 tonnes. But the port is still holding its own.'

The Port Authority directly employs 150 people, with a further 2,500 employed within the harbour area by a number of firms. The natural shelter of the Tay estuary and the fast flow of its deep waters keep the harbour free of silt and minimise the need for dredging.

'One big advantage of our location is that we can have comings and goings in the port 24 hours a day,' says Captain Watson. 'We are not a tidal port like Perth. The Tay is one of the few estuarial rivers that does not have a problem with dredging. It is one of the clearest estuaries in Europe and the problem of silt building up is minimal. But a hydrological survey of the sandbanks on the lower Tay is regularly carried out and we do keep a wary eye on them. Modern methods allow a very accurate prediction of sandbank movement and computers can process information quickly so it is easier to plan ahead. The maintenance work on channels and sandbanks is proactive rather than reactive. In the past, the problems of the Tay essentially arose because of lack of information.'

The commercial cut and thrust of competition for business keeps Captain Watson busy but he still has time to be reflective and speaks for many who live by and work on the Tay estuary when he declares, 'It is the environment of the Tay which makes the job so attractive. The clean air and water is refreshing and I think places where water flows will always fascinate people. Dreams can easily start on rivers which grow into careers. The waterside here is relaxing but you also see the anger of the water as well. To paraphrase an old sailor's saying, – "respect the river but never fear it".'

The Dundee fishing fleet in port, c.1900

Chapter II

DUNDEE: FROM JUTEOPOLIS TO CAMPUS CITY

Sprawling out from its ancient heart around the harbour, Dundee enjoys one of the finest estuarine settings of any European city. It has grown to embrace the former villages of Broughty Ferry and Invergowrie and its waterfront straddles seven miles of the north bank of the Tay. What was once a grim industrial fortress brooding under a thick blanket of smog from the hundreds of jute mill smokestacks has blossomed into a garden city, its fine parks and gardens complemented by awe-inspiring views of the river and the hills of Fife.

For many Scots, Dundee is an enigma, an industrial enclave more evocative of the West of Scotland, yet surrounded by the soft Angus countryside. The venue of an occasional important football match, political corruption scandal or industrial dispute, and home of William Topaz McGonagall and Dundee Cake, the city rarely intrudes on the national consciousness other than in news items registering another chapter of its industrial decline. There is little excuse for such ignorance and the principal reason for the mystery about Dundee is that, in the past, too few Scots have bothered to visit the place. That is now changing; and those who do take the road (and the miles) to Dundee are frequently surprised at the quality of life on offer, a factor which often persuades those who come to study or work to adopt the city as their home. For them it really is the 'City of Discovery' enthusiastically promoted by the city's marketing people.

Since the early 1980s Dundee has successfully fought to dispel the air of self-apology which once hung over the city like a toxic cloud. The poison of pessimism has been replaced with a renewed sense of self-confidence and a stoicism in the face of economic adversity. Dundonians are now eager to celebrate what is best in their history and to congratulate themselves on surviving the worst.

If Dundee ever was simply a city of 'jute, jam and journalism', it is now a centre of education, engineering and electronics, and is rapidly becoming a bright and modern campus city. King Jute may have ruled supreme in Dundee for almost a hundred years but this was never a city to be written off casually as 'the biggest village in Scotland'. Human settlement in the area dates from the prehistoric era when a fishing village was located at what is now the Stannergate. Later, during Roman times, Dundee became a centre of resistance to the invaders and a meeting place for Scottish and Pictish kings who united to repel the Romans.

Gradually its importance grew as a trading port with the countries of northern Europe, and in 1189 William the Lion granted the town its first Royal Charter. Dundee expanded rapidly in the twelfth and thirteenth centuries. Its prosperous merchants realised the importance of education and the Dundee Grammar School was founded, probably early in the thirteenth century. The school's most prominent pupil was William Wallace, the champion of Scottish independence, who cut short his studies to flee the city after killing the son of the English governor. Later, young men from Dundee were sent to distant Bologna to study the Roman law which governed Catholic Scotland. Dundee's political importance was also growing, its prosperity making it a prize which was taken on four occasions by English armies during the Wars of Independence.

By 1645, when the town was sacked and pillaged by the Marquis of Montrose, Dundee's population had grown to around 10,000. It was a cosmopolitan community with a keen awareness of the international political rivalries of the time which could explode locally with devastating results. No episode was more devastating for Dundee than the sacking of the city by Cromwell's troops in 1651. By now the second wealthiest town in Scotland, the local inhabitants put up a stiff resistance to the English forces commanded by General Monck. Dundee paid a heavy price for its support of the Royalist cause. The city governor and garrison were besieged in the Old Steeple, which still stands in the High Street; when they surrendered they were massacred along with many of Dundee's civilian population and much of the city was put to the torch.

During the Reformation, Dundee's willingness to embrace new and 'foreign' ideas was demonstrated when its enthusiasm for the Protestant cause earned it the title of 'Scotland's Geneva' and the cargoes from the Low Countries included reforming tracts. A century and a half later, Dundee was a hotbed of democratic discontent inspired by the ideals of the French revolutionaries with whom radical Dundonians had personal links. In the 1790s a tradition of maverick, independent radicalism was established which later saw the election of George Kinloch — who had been outlawed for his role in democratic agitation — as the city's first Member of Parliament. Dundee boasted a strong Chartist movement during the 'Hungry 1840s' and the traditional meeting place of the radicals on Magdalen Green overlooking the Tay even witnessed an attempt to start an insurrection and General Strike to win the vote. In a city where women workers were employed on a vast scale, the later suffragette movement also had a substantial following. Most famously, the city first elected the young Winston Churchill as a Liberal MP and then dumped him when he turned Tory — in favour of Neddy Scrymgeour, a Christian Socialist and the only Prohibitionist ever to be elected to the House of Commons. In the same election, of 1923, Dundee returned E. D. Morel, one of the country's most outspoken, and persecuted, pacifists during the First World War. More recently, Dundee in typically defiant and dissenting mood, provided the only urban refuge for the Scottish National Party during the 1970s and 1980s.

By the end of the nineteenth century 'Juteopolis' had grown to become what was arguably Europe's largest industrial monoculture, with half the city's population directly employed in the textile trade. The great bales of hemp which were carried halfway around the world from India were modern Dundee's first strength — and its greatest weakness: the city's primacy in jute gradually became a crippling dependency on an underinvested industry which was doomed to be undercut by the primary producers of the Indian sub-continent. It was, however, replaced by the man-made textiles in which Dundee is still a leader. The city has yet to recover fully from the phenomonen that was jute, though, and Dundee's collective psychology still bears the scars.

Nevertheless, it was jute, the successor to a vibrant linen industry, which allowed Dundee's population to soar faster than that of any other Scottish city. In just 60 years, from 1821 to 1881, it grew from 38,000 to 158,000. By the end of the nineteenth century the figure stood at 190,000, with 40,000 workers employed in the mills. Jute was a bonanza. As the Irish immigrants fleeing starvation crowded cheek by jowl with dispossessed Highlanders into the slums of the Overgate and Hawkhill, Dundee became a boisterous frontier town where the only thing lower than the average life expectancy was the cost of labour.

The poverty, even in good times, was appalling. In the bad times it was unimaginable. No other Scottish city was as heavily industrialised as Dundee. In 1911, for example, two thirds of Dundee's workforce was employed in manufacturing compared with only a half of that of Glasgow. When the Depression came, textiles and engineering were the first casualties; unemployment figures for July 1932 show a massive 37,000 Dundonians out of work. Unemployment in Dundee for that year stood at a crippling 35 per cent compared with a Scottish average of 22 per cent. In Dundee the 1930s really were 'hungry' but so were the 1920s and, before that, many of the decades of depression in the last century.

In Dundee, the rich man was in his 'Jute Palace' and the poor man – or more often woman – was kept firmly at the mill gate. The contrast between rich and poor could not have been more striking. In 1832 a House of Commons select committee reported on Dundee's factory conditions. It found that children from the age of six or seven started work at 3 a.m. and laboured until 10 p.m. To keep them awake during their 19-hour shift, the children were continually strapped by overseers. In his *Chapters in the Life of a Dundee Factory Boy*, James Myles recalled: 'The lash of the slave driver was never more sparingly used in Carolina on the unfortunate slave than the canes and "whangs" of the mill foremen were used on helpless factory boys.' Ruthless exploitation was also extended to adults. At the Strathmartine Mill on the northern outskirts of Dundee, foremen had their watches smashed by masters who threatened them for 'letting the hands know the time of day'.

The use of half-time child labour was widespread in the Dundee mills. In 1901 some 17 per cent of children aged 10 to 14 were in paid occupations compared with only 4.5 per cent of the same age group in Glasgow. It was desperation which drove the poor to mills, which were indeed dark and satanic. In 1851 a contemporary account revealed that 'the women spinners are all up in arms against the Spinning Mills and tell their daughters if they go to the Mills they will never get a Husband, they tell their sons that they lose their hands or even their life itself by going to the Mills'. The women knew what they were talking about: the working and social conditions of the Dundee millworkers was a national scandal which persisted up to the turn of this century. When recruiting sergeants appealed for volunteers for the Boer War in 1901, they found the undernourished Dundee volunteers around three inches shorter than the national average and several pounds lighter. Up to the Second World War, it was the common practice of the Dundee police to recruit stout country chiels to keep the diminutive Dundee weavers in order.

If Dundee's textile industry allowed thousands to subsist, it also, in the case of a tiny few, created powerful dynasties. Flax, processed in Dundee since the 1790s, was the basis for the fortune of one such family. When Britannia ruled the waves and the writ of the British Empire was enforced by the largest navy the world has ever known, it was the giant works of the Baxter family which supplied the canvas sails and gun covers. The Napoleonic Wars, the Crimean War and the American Civil War created huge demand for Baxter products and ensured enormous profits. Today the family is remembered by the park named after it, and the lower Dens works which have been turned into an award-winning housing development. In the Dundee of the 1840s, the Baxters were typical of the wealthy textile families. They were a force to be reckoned with and enjoyed amazing power. In his *History of the Working Classes in Scotland*, Tom Johnston, Labour's first Scottish Secretary and a one-time Dundee MP, records a case which was raised in Parliament: 'Six factory girls in the employment of Messrs Baxter, their ages from 14 to 20, and their wages being five shillings and sixpence per week, had the audacity to ask for an increase of a half-penny a day. The request was refused. After dinner they did not return to work and by the rules of the mill could have been fined time and a half for under time; but next morning Mr Baxter, instead of fining the girls, had them arrested and marched through the streets under police escort to a private office where was seated a magistrate, one of the Baxter family, and the overseer and the manager of the mill. The judicial Baxter there and then sentenced the girls to 10 days' hard labour!' Little wonder that Peter Carmichael, a partner in the Baxter firm, could write without fear of exaggeration that 'The Dens Works have been better than a gold mine'.

Gradually jute took over in importance from flax, in the process earning huge fortunes for the mill owners. The profits wrung from the mills were poured into overseas investment. The financial trust movement was born in Dundee and financed the opening up of the American West by investing in Texan cattle ranches and the railroads which helped to unite the USA. As the pioneers moved west, they did so in wagons covered with Dundee canvas. The First Scottish American Trust was launched in 1873 by Robert Fleming (a family name that remains influential in banking circles and also one which produced the creator of James Bond) and within ten years assorted trusts founded in Dundee raised a phenomenal £5 million, a vast sum in today's terms. The scale of the wealth accumulated by the textile barons was stunning. When jute was at its zenith, Broughty Ferry was reputed to be the 'richest square mile in the world' because of the number of millionaire inhabitants. The elaborate Italianate façades of some of the surviving mill buildings and the remaining 'Jute Palaces' of the jutocracy in Broughty Ferry and Dundee's west end are the visible memorials to Juteopolis.

The occasional jute ship still arrives at Dundee's harbour, but the industry is a faint shadow of its former self. Only about a thousand people are employed making specialist products; today's children are strangers to the ubiquitous strands of hemp which once blew around Dundee's streets like tumbleweed, just as adults are blind to the sign language which evolved in the mills to defeat the clatter of the looms. It was the concern felt by some Dundonians that this unique heritage might be lost forever that led to the foundation, in 1985, of the Dundee Heritage Trust. In response to the news that Dundee's College of Technology was to close its textiles department, a group of individuals took out personal overdrafts to purchase the department's collection of jute equipment.

That same year, the Trust appointed Jonathan Bryant, the former director of the Yorkshire Mining Museum, as chief executive. His first priority was to oversee the return of RRS *Discovery* to its home base. The Trust is responsible for the administration and running of the *Discovery*; the ship has now moved to what will be its final resting place at Discovery Point where it has a custom-built visitor centre to graphically outline the vessel's history and times.

With *Discovery* safely ensconced in its new berth Jonathan and his team are now reconstructing an old Dundee jute mill at the Verdant Works. He explains: 'The idea for the Trust came from the fact that people in the community were not comfortable at the prospect of nothing of the city's trades and industry being retained for future generations. Dundee Heritage Trust and its operational organisation, Dundee Industrial Heritage, were set up to give a proper legal and financial structure. Both are charities which aim to preserve and present the industrial heritage of Dundee for the public benefit.

'The collection of jute equipment could have been put in a modern low-cost building, but we felt that it is not just the technical side of industry that is important. We want to capture a way of life and the fabric of the industry as well. You can only really understand an industry in the context of the buildings and the people who worked in them. While looking for a suitable building, we had a couple of false starts. Then the opportunity to bring the *Discovery* to Dundee came along and we couldn't say no to that. That delayed our textile project but we returned to it, determined to find a suitable listed building. The criteria for finding a place for the jute equipment was not just a good or Grade A building. We needed a range of spaces to illustrate the whole process. When looking at places we had to ask ourselves whether it had a yard, a boilerhouse, a chimney, preparing areas, spinning areas and so on.'

Salvation finally came in the shape of an old mill used as a scrapyard and funding from an unusual source. Jonathan recalls, 'A number suggested themselves but Verdant Works was typical of the most famous mills in Dundee. It was sixteenth in terms of volume production and it employed four hundred people. It is typical of a middle-rank mill. We eventually secured Verdant Works with a 100 per cent grant of £100,000 from the National Heritage Memorial Fund in London. It came as a shock to some people that this body put a jute works in the same category as a Rembrandt!

'We acquired the works in 1991 and did wind and water-tightening work on it to save it from further deterioration. Money was raised for the refurbishment of the period offices and we formed the Verdant Works Committee. We have set out a development plan and are now actively fund-raising. The Works have been open to the public since June 1992 but we are progressing each part of the project at a time, as funds become available.'

Jonathan has some sympathy for the view that keeping remnants of the industrial past for visitors to gawp at can verge on the voyeuristic but he believes that it is vital for a community to retain something to illustrate its roots and to provide a point of interest and understanding for visitors to the area. 'It is important that people know where jute came from and what it became', he stresses. 'We're not going to set it up to be exactly like a jute mill. What we want to do is take examples of items in the appropriate areas and take people through the principles of jute production. We also want to show the various uses of the textile. Above all, it is an opportunity to underline jute's significance in the Dundee story. This industry employed a quarter of the city's population in 1900 – that is 50,000 people. As far as the people of what is now Bangladesh were concerned, Dundee was the centre of western civilisation. Jute made Dundee different from other places in Scotland. A phenomenon such as this is so significant that you can't afford to ignore it. Very few people in Dundee now work within the industry, but attitudes, environments and social structures are still based on the industry.'

The decline of jute and its consignment to a new role in Dundee's booming heritage industry has been mirrored by jam, Dundee's middle 'J'. Once famed for its sweets, Dundee Cake, Keiller's marmalade and the sweet jams made from the raspberries and strawberries of Gowrie and Strathmore, Dundee's confectionery tradition is now cherished and maintained at

Shaw's Sweetie Factory. It has become a tourist attraction in its own right as well as being a confectionery manufacturer. The factory, run by Englishman Derek Shaw, is a direct spin-off from the Keiller company, one-time producers of 'Dundee Marmalade' and is now the last reminder of a once proud industry. Taken over by a succession of multinational and large UK companies, Keiller's and its Dundee traditions became items on a distant balance-sheet and Derek Shaw opted to run his own business.

He explains his decision. 'This company has been going since 1988. Sweet-making is a tradition in my family which started in Kent in 1879. I left Kent many years ago and was eventually asked to run Keiller's. I think it's disgusting that Keiller's has gone. Those skills have been lost forever. It was a waste of a resource. Sweet-making was a strong tradition in Scotland. A lot of sugar came into Scotland, and Dundee was one of the main Commonwealth destinations for sugar exports. Once the sugar was here, you had jam and marmalade. There was a strong tradition in Dundee for over 200 years, and now we are the only people in the city who do this.'

Like so many incomers to Tayside, Derek was a ready convert to the Tay's life-style. 'With the decline of Keiller's, I decided to go back to my sweetie-making roots. When I left Keiller's I was offered fantastic jobs down south, but the quality of life and the people here appeal so much to me. We live in the village of Liff which is fantastic, within ten minutes I can be into the hills or down at the river. I lived in Kent, which is known as the "Garden of England", but I still had to travel 17 miles to my office, a journey that could take anything up to two hours. We put together the sweetie factory from scratch. Dundee has become a tourist centre and more people are stopping off in the city, so we felt it would be an opportunity to show off our skills. We produce 15 tonnes of sweets a week and in 1992 I estimate that we had 22,000 people visit the factory. The visitor goes on to a viewing gallery where they can see all the sweets being made and staff can explain to them what they are doing.

'That side of the business, providing a tourist attraction by making old-fashioned sweets, has succeeded by word of mouth. On the other side, I've got a business to run – which is the difficult bit. When I started up the recession was really just beginning. So I went abroad to get orders for exports. I got the plane for Holland then after that went to Germany and Scandinavia. I brought back orders and we concentrated on exports. We make very much the traditional sweet, which you can't produce on modern machines. It takes longer to make but it means we have complete flexibility and the quality control is tight. We make 160 different types of fudge. I think we are appealing to the nostalgia market. According to research, people want boiled sweets but they can't buy them. We package our sweets in polythene or cellophane bags to stop them going sticky, but people have asked for paper bags. They remember their sweets from childhood being sticky.'

It is journalism, alone among the three 'J's, that continues to flourish in Dundee. From its studios in the city Radio Tay broadcasts news and current affairs across 'Tay territory' and beyond. Grampian Television, BBC Scotland, *The Scotsman*, *Daily Record* and *Daily Express* all maintain a local presence. Above all, of course, Dundee is synonymous with D. C. Thomson & Co, publishers of the *Sunday Post*, the *Dundee Courier & Advertiser* and the *Evening Telegraph*, and launching-pad for scores of journalistic careers. The family-owned company is one of Dundee's largest private employers, with around 1,800 journalists, photographers, sub-editors, artists, secretaries, printers and drivers on its pay-roll in the city.

Evening 'Tele' *for sale, High Street, Dundee*

'D. C.s', as Thomson is universally referred to in Dundee, may have a lengthy history and some of its titles may appear ageless, but the company is at the forefront of printing and design technology. The firm's impressive red sandstone edifice at Meadowside in the city centre now houses state-of-the-art page make-up computer systems which are among the most advanced in the world. They are directly linked to huge modern printing presses, the product of a multi-million-pound investment programme by the company in new technology on Dundee's peripheral Kingsway.

The company produces a range of long-running titles, including *My Weekly* and *People's Friend*, both of which sell many hundreds of thousands of copies per issue, as well as newer titles such as *Catch* and *Shout* which are aimed at the younger female market. The firm's oldest product, the ever-popular *Scots Magazine*, can boast a pedigree stretching back to January 1739 when it was first published in Edinburgh by a partnership of two booksellers and two printers. It ran for 20 years without an editor and appeared in a similar size format to that of today. It then had an erratic history until 1927 when D. C. Thomson took it over and appointed James Salmond, a highly regarded writer, as editor. His reign lasted until 1948 and he encouraged twentieth-century literary names, including Hugh MacDiarmid and Lewis Grassic Gibbon, who were regular callers to the office.

Salmond was succeeded in 1949 by Arthur Daw who introduced outdoor, architectural, historical and contemporary articles to the magazine and moulded it into what it has become today. The formula was popular and the circulation took off, growing by tens of thousands and providing a monthly link with home for Scots expatriates around the world. The current editor is John Rundle, a former BBC *Superscot* champion who heads the team of four which produces the magazine. He explains, 'There has been very little change to Daw's formula. It has been a case of gradual change – evolution rather than revolution. Scots climber Tom Weir started to write a regular article each month in 1956. It was entitled "My Month" and is still in the magazine now. It is our longest-running feature.'

John stresses that the 300,000 readers of the *Scots Magazine* enjoy a special relationship with their magazine. 'The *Scots Magazine* is a little chunk of nostalgia for quite a few people. It is particularly popular with expatriates – our overseas sales are greater than the entire sales of its nearest competitor. The magazine is mailed to virtually every country in the world with the bulk of the sales going to Australia, Canada, New Zealand and the United States. The readers love the magazine. Scotland has a small population and there is a great feeling of familiarity. I think that the magazine fills the gaps that people discover as they grow older. English readers say that the magazine is marvellous and ask why there cannot be an English equivalent. But I doubt if they are as passionate about their country as the Scots are about theirs.'

Apart from serious journalism, D. C. Thomson is famous for its comics. Their characters have entertained generations of children brought up on the *Beano* and the *Dandy* and who eagerly waited for their parents to finish reading the *Sunday Post* each week in order to catch up with the adventures of Oor Wullie and the couthy Broons family. Some of the characters have attained an astonishing popularity. One of the best-loved creations of D. C. Thomson's 'Fun Factory' is the ageless Dennis the Menace who has made a weekly appearance in the *Beano* for over 40 years.

Euan Kerr has worked on the *Beano* since 1978 and, in 1984, was appointed editor. He is delighted to talk about the amazing following attracted to Dennis the Menace and Gnasher, his faithful canine companion. 'Dennis has become something of a phenomenon. The Dennis the Menace fan club was started in 1976 and now has over 1.25 million members with an average of eight hundred members enrolling each week. When we celebrated his fortieth anniversary, we promoted it with Dennis dressed in a tracksuit and shades. This was really seized on by the media but nobody realised that, at the end of the story, Dennis had had all of his new gear ripped by Gnasher and he was back to normal. Kids love rebellious characters who are anti-authority in a comic, timeless way. Kids tend not to wear shorts to school these days but nobody minds that *Beano* characters do. I would say that Dennis is very proud of his knobbly knees.'

Curiously, Britain has not been subjected to a demented cult of Dennis the Menace junior tearaways, partly because of the unique appeal of the *Beano* characters but also thanks to the care that is taken with story-lines. As the editor emphasises, 'In the 1950s, some parents looked on these anti-establishment characters with horror, but nowadays they are well accepted. We are very aware of social problems and of the responsibilities of our job. Our characters are very much exaggerated and they get to ham it up in stories. But they never mess with fireworks or anything like that, and if Dennis zooms around on rollerskates it is always in a park and not in the streets. There has been a change in approach to certain subjects, such as corporal punishment. Dennis used to be punished by his father with "the demon whacker", a large slipper, but that has now been dropped.'

Euan and four colleagues divide responsibility for characters between them and think up story-lines to be sent to a team of 15 to 18 trusted freelance artists for illustration. Harmony is developed between the writers and artists and every attempt is made to keep artists with the same characters. Returned pencil drawings are inked and the whole process from script to comic page takes around two months. The *Beano* first appeared in 1938 and has kept its position as Britain's leading comic, attracting five hundred readers' letters each week. So, in the age of the computer game, how does the *Beano* team maintain an appeal with children of today?

Euan explains: 'There was a Dennis puppet on satellite television a while ago. The puppet was great and the backgrounds were brilliant, but the problem was the voice. In the stories there are no hints of accent or specific geographical location. The *Beano*'s longevity is to do with the characters which sell the product. There are so many big names that it is difficult to improve on. Comics may not sell as well as they used to due to television and computers but since the fiftieth anniversary of the comic in 1988, we have moved into merchandising and there is a large range of spin-offs like summer specials, annuals, puzzle books and joke books involving *Beano* characters.

'There are many fads in the comic world which are just money-making devices with a high-intensity TV-linked sales pitch. We cannot predict these trends and our outlook is very different. We aim to produce an enduring comic and characters that will be around in 20 years' time. The *Beano* is very enjoyable to work on. In many ways you can remain a child for a long time. It gives me a lot of satisfaction to see all our hard work in print and it is a great source of pride to work on Britain's top comic. Who knows what the future will be like? But the *Beano* will go on.'

The computer age may represent a vague challenge to the *Beano*, but for some Dundonians it has been a positive opportunity. Fittingly, the city which gave Britain's children the Bash Street Kids in the 1950s is now producing a range of popular computer games in the 1990s that are selling in their millions. A lemming-like success may sound like a contradiction in terms but for one young Dundonian the suicidal habits of these furry rodents have inspired a bestselling game and opened up sensational horizons for his computer company. David Jones founded DMA Design in 1988 when he was just 22 years old, and the company's irresistible rise is the stuff of which capitalist fairytales are made.

As an apprentice electronics engineer, David learned his trade building Spectrum computers for Sir Clive Sinclair in Dundee's once giant Timex factory. Voluntary redundancy allowed him to take up a college course in computer sciences which he was never to finish. In his first year at college, David decided to try his hand at computer game design. A year later he had completed his first game and, to his delight, had it accepted by a publisher. Business now beckoned, and within four years the college drop-out could count ten of his former classmates among his staff of 22 – with an average age of just 24 years. Turnover broke through the £1 million barrier in 1992 and the business, solely owned by David, has twice had to move to bigger premises. He has also opened a retail 'softwarehouse' selling direct to the public, thus providing a ready-made market research facility. All in all, it has been an impressively smooth transition from working in a bedroom at home to a suite of smart offices in Dundee's Technology Park.

The *Lemmings* game sold over one million copies and earned a string of prestigious awards. Its successor, *Lemmings II*, looks set to follow suit. David has become the Stephen Hendry of the Scottish computer software industry. He has lost none of his passion for computer games and can scarcely believe his luck. 'There are times when this isn't really like a job,' he says. 'It all began when I bought a Commodore Amiga with part of my redundancy money. At that time these were fairly new machines and it took a year to complete my first game. It was called *Menace* and, when I brought it to a specialist games fair in London, a publisher took it up. It did really well and I involved some of my classmates in converting it for use on other systems. The second game I produced was *Blood Money* which sold 40,000 units. I decided to take a year out of my studies and see if I could make a go of it because the games were taking up most of my time and my college work was suffering. I've not been back to college since.'

It was *Lemmings*, the third game to be developed, which put David on the road to software stardom and even persuaded computer-game giant Nintendo to make a pilgrimage to Dundee. 'We launched *Lemmings* in February 1991,' David recalls, 'and on the launch day we shipped out one order of 50,000 units for Amiga. That was as many as we could have expected to sell over a year. After a push in the specialist magazines, the game basically sold itself and has been converted for use on all systems. A US company has developed the game for arcade-machine use. I understand this is a first, because it is usually arcade games that are developed for home use and not the other way around.' The attraction of the game, he believes, lies in its simplicity. 'It gets progressively harder, but you always know that you can do it. Then there's the satisfaction of knowing that you have saved the lemmings – it is a non-violent game.'

DMA is typical of a range of hi-tech firms in Dundee – from multinationals like National Cash Register producing most of the world's automatic telling-machines to small computer software companies – in recognising the importance of research and development. Unlike the jute firms and contract engineering factories of old, there is no question of resting on any laurels at DMA. As its youthful owner explains, 'We have got to have the edge on fierce competition, so research and development is very important to us. The next development will probably be compact disc game systems and it will be best to be in on that early. These will be like small CD films and will be complicated and expensive to design.'

DMA is one of the finest examples of a rash of young hi-tech and biotech businesses which have sprung up on the city's industrial estates, often as a spin-off from Dundee's burgeoning educational sector. The city's student population is well over 10,000. The merger of the University of Dundee with the Duncan of Jordanstone College of Art will create a major new force in Scottish education with a student population of 6,000 and an established leadership in fields as diverse as biochemistry, civil engineering, law and dentistry. The Dundee Institute of Technology is expanding and, with a wide range of degree courses on offer, is continuing its campaign for university status. The city's future as a campus city with an emphasis on vocational courses seems secure. The teaching hospital at Ninewells is at the forefront of cancer research, attracting scientists in ever greater numbers to what has become a recognised centre of excellence in combatting the disease.

In recent years Dundee has emerged, too, as a significant distribution centre, and firms in a number of industries have been able to take advantage of the city's equidistant position between Scotland's major cities. The English may be a nation of shopkeepers but they could learn a thing or two from Dundonians. The Tayside city is the headquarters of three of Britain's most important food distributors: Watson and Philip, C. J. Lang and William Low have grown from local beginnings to straddle Britain with a combined turnover of over £1 billion.

When Hugh MacDiarmid described the Dundee of the 1930s as a 'grim industrial cul-de-sac,' not even the city's most evangelical admirers could have disputed the poet's view of the smog-ridden slums with the mill chimney stacks punctuating the grey skyline like dozens of exclamation marks. Even the most optimistic would have doubted Dundee's ability to generate a tourist industry, and yet, over the last decade, the city has done just that. Dundee is now recognised as a pleasant conference centre and a convenient base for touring holidays of Tayside region. The city has upgraded and added to its hotel and restaurant amenities. The

Municipal astronomer, Dr Fiona Vincent

45

refurbished McManus Galleries house a fine art gallery and museum. Camperdown Park boasts a wildlife centre which allows children access to some of the animals and the Heritage Centre at Discovery Point brings the story of Dundee to life by using the latest museum techniques.

One of the city's oddest attractions is the Mills Observatory on Balgay Hill. It overlooks the Tay and is supervised by Britain's only full-time municipal astronomer. According to Dr Fiona Vincent, 'Mills Observatory was not designed to give a view of the city and surrounding countryside. Our interest is in looking upwards through the telescope. But because of the position of the observatory on one of the highest points in Dundee, we can see most of the city and the countryside from telescopes placed on the balcony. We can look down the Tay with our telescopes and get some really cracking views of the seals on the sandbanks. The geese which fly over Invergowrie Bay make another impressive sight. The river's seasonal activities can be well observed from here. Although most of Dundee is urbanised, the fact that river and countryside can be seen from around the city is a real bonus. Even when your main interest is the sky above, there is no escaping the beauty and drama of the countryside in which you are located. To the south we can see as far as the Pentland Hills and to the north we can see the Grampians.

'The middle of a city isn't really an ideal position for an observatory, because of all the problems of heat and light. But this is the only fully public observatory in Britain, so it has to be on a city site so the public can utilise it. We get visitors all the time – around 15,000 a year. School parties use the facilities during the day and at nights we get societies from a whole range of activities coming for a talk or to look at the stars through a telescope. We have a planetarium which is used as an educational device but can come in handy if there's too much cloud around.

'The river is a major influence on the atmosphere around it. Because such a large body of water takes a long time to either cool down or heat up, there is a regular, steady air temperature above it. The tides are influenced by the position of the moon. We check the tides of the river to make sure that they are correct according to moon activity, and I'm happy to say that the Tay does concur with moon activity. At the new moon and full moon there is a very noticeable change, and the river is at its highest and then lowest at these times.'

Below Balgay Hill, sandwiched between the spectacular jute palaces of Perth Road and the reclaimed land at Riverside – now home to Dundee Airport – lie the Botanic Gardens of Dundee University, another hidden gem among the city's tourist attractions. An oasis of tranquility just minutes from the city centre, this working garden is a valued haven for those with an interest in plants or those merely seeking peace and quiet. Hothouses recreate the conditions of arid desert and steamy jungle, and an imaginatively designed visitor centre houses exhibitions and displays. The walks among the conifers, birches and more exotic eucalyptus afford breathtaking views over the river to the Kingdom of Fife.

Curator Leslie Bisset emphasises that the gardens are not there just to look good: 'The botanic gardens were started by the University in 1971 as a teaching establishment. The garden is situated in the curve of the Sidlaws to the north-west of the garden and this shelters us from the wind. We are influenced by the river in topological matters but are far enough away not to be affected by salt-laden winds. Because of the situation of the garden we borrow heavily from the landscape of the river and of Fife in our layout.

'The garden has been created on what were disused fields, on top of rock-vaulted fellside with sandstone intrusions which is a rarity in the UK. When we dig down in the garden we come to river gravel which is a curious mixture of reddish sandstone and alluvial-rich soil. The

Leslie Bisset in the Botanic Gardens

ground is fairly water-retentive and is a good load-bearing soil. This is good from a management point of view, but it makes digging with spades difficult. The layout of the garden is primarily to service the needs of students. I believe that the Dundee University Botanic Gardens have a great deal of integrity and relevance about them. Our core functions extend beyond providing a "pretty garden" and we want the kind of visitor who is interested in more than gimmicks. The botanic garden in Dundee has a lot more purpose than many in Britain. We deal in plant associations and habitats and try to read landscapes. The garden is interested in the biology of plants rather than the naming of them; we are more concerned with what they do rather than what they are. After ten years at the gardens I am still surprised at what can grow here, and the rate of growth.'

The botanic gardens have become a part of the university's 'town and gown' strategy of integrating the groves of academe with the community, and visitors are welcome. As Leslie explains, 'The natural landscapes laid out in the garden try to provide for the ecosystems of the plants. Our method of layout is natural and economic to maintain. The centre of the city could learn a lot from us about this. Town landscaping is too false and needs a high manpower rate to maintain it. We get around 10,000 visitors a year and are able to provide hands-on experience for school parties. We try to show children ecological niches rather than provide "living dodos" for them to look at. Pointing out the general malaise that is occurring in the

environment is a vital part of our work in conservation, and we collect and distribute rare seeds.'

Dundee, diversified and 'discovered', has come a long way since the days when the 'three J's' was a covenient short-hand phrase to describe the city of the inter-war years, but there was always much more to the city than simply jute, jam and journalism. For a start there were the people and their tremendous spirit of community and hope which, as the phenomenon that was jute declined, emerged as Dundee's true strength.

Partly as a result of their town's relative geographical isolation, Dundee's citizens have made their own entertainment, allowing a unique culture to emerge. Over the past decade the city has undergone a cultural voyage of self-discovery, and some would say that Dundee has been reclaimed by Dundonians now confident in their own identity. Public arts programmes inspired by Dundee's past have enlivened run-down areas and provided a model for urban regeneration in other parts of Britain. The city has produced some of the country's largest community theatre projects, involving thousands of Dundonians, and live music is performed in clubs and pubs on a greater scale than anywhere else in Scotland. Ricky Ross of Deacon Blue, Billy MacKenzie of The Associates, Danny Wilson and Michael Marra are just a few of the talented musicians to emerge from the city in recent years.

Perhaps only in Dundee would a group of ordinary folk with little or no musical experience have the enthusiasm, courage and nerve to form their own 'orchestra'. Self-styled 'tunesmith' Kevin Murray, a talented composer and musician with a passionate belief in Dundee, was as surprised as anyone at the emergence of the People's Orchestra of Dundee – for which he now works as resident composer and musical director.

'The People's Orchestra started in 1989,' he recounts. 'It grew out of a community play that I was doing called *The Mystery Play*. We made up a band of community players and the music was committed to tape with a recording of *The Mystery Play* in the Caird Hall. Afterwards, a crowd of people gathered round the piano and asked, "What's next?". We have been meeting twice a week ever since. The whole intention of the People's Orchestra is that I write to people's strengths with their weaknesses in mind. It is quality music to exploit their best angle. There are 28 registered members of the orchestra and we aim to recruit more. Some members were non-musical before but everyone in the orchestra can now read treble and bass clef. Early on we decided that the orchestra should give ordinary people the chance to work with high-class professionals, an opportunity that they would not otherwise get, and the People's Orchestra has performed with the Scottish Chamber Orchestra and also with jazz saxophonist Tommy Smith.'

Four years after being founded, the People's Orchestra is going from strength to strength and Kevin believes it is following in a well-established musical tradition in Dundee. 'The local branch of the Musician's Union, of which I am proud to be the chairperson, was the first in Britain and celebrated its centenary in 1993. The National Music Day celebrations in Dundee were the biggest per head of population in Britain, with 29 different events on in the city. Dundee has produced proportionately more songwriters than Glasgow and has a very rich culture. The problem is that we do not have a proper cultural policy or infrastructure to support young talent. I have seen too many people signing contracts and losing out.'

Having abandoned a promising career as a session musician to pursue his passion for composing, Kevin is concerned to write music which is contemporary but melodic, harmonic

PREVIOUS PAGE: A Dundee cityscape

and, above all, accessible. Inspired as a youngster by Jimmy Deuchars, the legendary Dundee jazz musician of world-class status, Kevin is determined that ordinary people should have access to the world of music. He has written and composed *Fitba*, a 'football opera', and a major work inspired by the Tay which has enjoyed a second run at the Dundee Rep and attracted critical acclaim.

'*The Salmon's Tail* was written about a ghillie catching his "biggest fish ever",' explains Kevin. He spends his whole life fishing and dies trying to catch one, only to be reincarnated as a salmon. I have fished the Tay for years and got the idea for the opera when I was working as a ghillie with Stan Pelc, a ghillie at Dunkeld, who served as a model for the main character. Since I wrote the play, I've not had the heart to take a fish out of the river.'

The Duncan of Jordanstone College of Art, Scotland's largest art college, has played an important part in developing Dundee's visual arts scene. Dundee paved the way in developing public arts in Scotland and the location of the British Healthcare Arts Centre at the college is testament to Dundee's lead in this field. Throughout the 1960s and 1970s the art college grew under the stewardship of Alberto Morrocco and now has a deserved reputation for textile design, jewellery, electronic imaging and television production, fine art and architecture.

Many students opt to stay in Dundee, seduced by its warmth and friendliness, and encouraged by its lack of pretentiousness. One such former student is public art pioneer Bob McGilvray, who recalls the early days of the programme which has tranformed Dundee's environment and lifted its spirits: 'We went out to dispel the idea of the artist as distant and isolated from the community, working in a garret. The art element in Blackness, the first area we targeted, is incorporated in the overall design and not just something which has been stuck on. We made art as much a part of the area's refurbishment as the bricks and mortar. That meant the artists worked alongside the architects and engineers at an early stage.'

Bob observes that Dundee has changed beyond all recognition since he arrived in 1970 to take up a place at Duncan of Jordanstone. As exhibitions organiser of the successful independent Seagate Gallery, he is well placed to comment on the state of the visual arts in the city: 'Prior to 1986 Dundee did not have a contemporary art gallery in the city centre and there was a good deal of scepticism when Dundee Printmakers moved into an old whisky bond with the help of the Arts Council and Dundee District Council. It was said that contemporary art would not sell in the city, but that has proved to be wrong. Good work and good marketing ensure that we are selling artworks and our figures have shown a healthy trend.'

He stresses the surprising level of local support for major contemporary exhibitions. The avant-garde 'Living Paintings' show began its Scottish tour in Dundee and attracted 8,000 visitors. There have been similar turnouts for exhibitions by sculptor David Mach and photographer Calum Colvin, both of whom graduated locally. The arts have been further strengthened by the establishment of the Meadow Mill, a thriving colony of 50 studios in an old jute mill, now home to dozens of painters, potters, sculptors and designers. It offers low rents and a sense of community to young artists, many of whom have just graduated from the nearby art college.

For all of the advances in contemporary art, most Dundonians would instantly give one name if asked to identify a prominent living artist. Dr James McIntosh Patrick was born the son of a Dundee architect in 1907 and is now Scotland's leading landscape artist. Apart from his studies at Glasgow School of Art – where he was one of the most gifted students in the class

James McIntosh Patrick in his studio

of 1924 – and his war service, the painter has spent all his life by the Tay, which he lovingly refers to as 'that majestic river'. His beloved river features in his best-known work, *Tay Bridge from my Studio Window*, a view from his house overlooking the historic Magdalen Green which was painted in 1948 and has changed little since. His landscapes, sometimes criticised for being quaint or idealised, are firm favourites with local people and prints adorn the walls of thousands of homes in Tayside and beyond. In his home territory of Tayside he is immensely popular. There is normally a waiting-list of about 40 for his oil paintings, with demand far outstripping supply. Often farmers and lairds who come across McIntosh Patrick immortalising their landscapes will buy his work straight off the easel. Hunched over a canvas on a farm track, puffing on a cigar, and clad in a deerstalker and tweed jacket, the artist has become as much a part of the Tayside scenery as the landscape he has captured on canvas and popularised worldwide.

The artist is the first to admit he has been a fortunate man. 'I have lived in my house, a Georgian-style mansion, here by the river for over 50 years and wake up to a view of the river every day. It is a sight that I will never tire of. It is a fantastic stretch of water which is surrounded by wonderful scenery. I particularly enjoy the river at night when you can see the twinkling lights of Fife and the hazard lamps on the rail bridge. The river is enjoyable because it changes so much; the variety of tides make it like the sea. The Tay has been quite inspirational in my painting and is hard to get away from if you are painting this area. It always seems to crop up in view.'

Modest about his considerable talents, McIntosh Patrick believes that his surroundings have been a significant factor in his success and, despite spending almost six decades painting the land of the Tay, he has lost none of his enthusiasm for the area. 'The whole countryside around here has been my real inspiration. The Tay valley and the hills around Strathmore provide Dundee with a wonderful hinterland. Villages like Rait and Abernyte on the north bank of the Tay interest me greatly. These are built on the contours of the land and afford some wonderful views.

'The river creeps into my pictures as a strip in the distance or in the shape of one of its marvellous tributaries with their little bridges and stone-built farmhouses. The setting of the river also helps me to compose my paintings of certain views and gives a good contrast. The landscape around Dundee is wonderfully rich and contains fine trees which are a joy to paint. I like a landscape where man's hands have smoothed things out, where there are small dykes and bridges and trees between fields. Now things are too mechanised. I miss the corn-stooks and wheat-stacks which I used to paint and am nostalgic for. There are less dry-stane dykes too; when you looked at those you could imagine the men laying all the stones together. These things were lovely to look at and added so much to the landscape. It is a pity that much in the countryside is now run down – but nothing can detract from the beauty that is all around us here in Dundee.'

Over the years hundreds of local people have attended art classes taught by a man who has been happy to pass on his knowledge of painting and deep appreciation of the countryside. Not only has the painter enjoyed the fantastic quality of life available in Dundee, he has added to it himself. 'I hope that my paintings have heightened people's awareness of the wonders that surround them. The flat land of the Carse is like something out of Holland and has such a low horizon with the Tay if, that is, you can possibly ignore the hills. The great variety of scenery by the Tay is a real joy. The changing seasons and different times of day and year give the countryside a whole fresh meaning for me. I have centred my art on this area and still paint every day.'

Central to Dundee's culture is sport and, as in any other Scottish city, football especially. Long-distance runner Liz McColgan and boxer Dick McTaggart are two of the best-known names produced by a city which has more than its fair share of swimming, boxing, athletics, rugby and amateur football clubs. Remarkably, despite a population which is declining at the rate of 2,000 a year to its current figure of 170,000, Dundee has also been able to sustain – although not without some difficulty – two rival Premier League football clubs.

For over 20 years Jim McLean's name has been synonymous with football in Dundee. Once memorably reminded by a Scottish sports writer that he was 'a joiner from Falkirk and not a carpenter from Nazareth', his tenure as manager of Dundee United has been colourful and eventful, and above all, highly successful. In 1993, though going on to become chairman of his club, McLean announced his retiral as manager of the team which he has built up over 21 years. Scotland's longest-serving manager can look back on a career which saw United win the Premier League in 1982–83 and reach the European Cup semi-final in 1984 and the final of the UEFA cup in 1987. Sometimes criticised for his fiery temperament, Jim has created the conditions which allowed United to play in Europe for 14 seasons. He is also responsible for the stability which encouraged former star player Paul Sturrock to stay on and coach at the club, and David Narey to win deserved recognition as one of the longest-serving players in the Scottish League. Club captain Maurice Malpas, furthermore, is only one of the United players to win a regular place in the Scotland team.

During his years at Tannadice Jim has developed a loyalty not just to United but also to the city of Dundee and, as he looks back on his career, he clearly regards the United supporters as having made it all worthwhile: 'There have definitely been changes during my time here. We are a far more widely respected club through our European experience. The club had a couple of magnificent results in the past and we've had a few similar experiences in my time. That has been good for the club, the supporters and the city. The supporters received a Fair Play award for their behaviour at the UEFA Cup final and that made me very proud. It was the first time it had ever been presented, and the United fans deserved it. There is a healthy rivalry between Dundee and Dundee United but it has never been about religion and there are no problems between the fans.'

He feels that supporters should be rewarded for their loyalty not just with more entertaining football and better results, but also with better facilities: 'For far too long, supporters have been taken for granted. In the present era people have much more choice in what to do with their money leisure-wise. I was pleased to witness the construction of the new viewing boxes, the demolition of the old covered enclosure and the erection of the new stand in its place. We also now provide hospitality facilities for business people and we have new lounges. This is all money that has had to be spent and there is still a lot to do. I would like to see new stands behind the top goal and the bottom goal but this will take a lot of money.'

Jim's high expectations of his players both on and off the pitch are legendary. In an era when price-tags of millions of pounds can be applied to young players, and turn their heads in the process, these have earned Jim a reputation as a tough boss and strict disciplinarian but he defends his position: 'Through football, the people and the city of Dundee have without doubt been recognised all over Europe. It is important to me that every time a player steps out on to the street, he should be a walking advertisement for the club and the city. Travelling abroad, it is important to set the right example. The players and the supporters are ambassadors for the city.'

He is firm in his belief, too, that the United team must be restored to its former glory and that the future of the side lies with the next generation. 'I believe that if we are to get the team back into a challenging position both here and in Europe, youth policy will be a very important factor,' he says. 'We cannot buy the quality we need because of our resources, so we get top-class players by rearing them. There can be gaps. In the David Narey era there were a lot of players in a group at that time including John Holt, Raymond Stewart, Paul Sturrock and David Dodds – it was a tremendous group at that time. We also have good groups of 19 and 13-year-olds now. We take kids from anywhere and have centres all over the country. If we were dependent on Dundee alone to find young talent we would never be near the top of the game.

'The future of United is to get back to where we were. It will take hard work to win trophies and return to Europe to spread the gospel of Dundee city and its people. I love living in Dundee. That's the reason why I didn't take other jobs that were offered. I love living in Broughty Ferry. I come from the West of Scotland and I appreciate life on the East Coast. East of Scotland supporters are far more refined and not as crude or loud as West Coast supporters. I want our supporters as loud but not as brash.'

Less than a hundred yards from Jim's office, Dens Park – the home of United's local rivals, Dundee FC – provides employment for another West Coaster who is just as enthusiastic about the merits of Dundee and its football culture. Jim Duffy combines the role of assistant manager with that of player at Dens where Dundee's senior club is struggling to re-establish itself as a major force in Scottish football. His career has witnessed two earlier spells with the dark blues between playing for Celtic and Morton, and a string of managerial positions with Airdrie, Falkirk and Partick Thistle.

When the opportunity arose to return to Tayside in May 1992, Jim Duffy had few qualms about accepting the post: 'People have said to me that Dundonians keep themselves to themselves, but I found the opposite to be the case. The supporters made me feel very welcome. I met a few friends through time and they all made me feel comfortable in the city. During my first spell here my daughter was born at Ninewells. Kim is now five and she is back in Dundee. I feel great affection for the place and the club. A testimonial match was held for me in Dundee in 1987 against a league select team with a lot of talent. My career was virtually finished then, due to a knee injury. Medical opinion was that I'd not play again and I was told to give up for the good of my long-term health. I gave up for two and a half years, but the bug got me again and I feel now that I'm doing okay.'

Jim has returned to Dundee during a controversial period which has seen a change of ownership and a public debate about the city's ability to support two clubs. Nonetheless, he is optimistic: 'Over the last 15 years Dundee FC has been remade many times, which has made things difficult. Dundee United has had stability and continuity, which Dundee has not had. Changes can be reflected on the football park but I believe we are more consistent on all levels now, from the boardroom down, and that will be reflected in the results. There are new people in charge now: Chairman Ron Dixon has made a major investment in the club. Dundee FC now has Czech, Dutch, Danish and several English players in the team – and there are one or two Scots in there as well! We are playing against the best clubs in the country. In August 1992 we had a great game at Dens which gave us a 4–3 victory against Rangers. They had enjoyed an unbeaten run since January and people assumed that, as we were a new side, the result would be the other way. But the fans were right behind us that day and the players rose to the occasion. The passion and commitment of the players allied to the passion and commitment of the fans made for a great day. It was a throwback to years ago. Rangers had a phenomenal record and our supporters really enjoyed that game. We had beaten the best team in the country where the English champions, Leeds United, could not.'

Like his rival across the road, Jim is a firm devotee of the Dundee lifestyle. 'I am delighted to be here,' he says. 'I enjoy living in Broughty Ferry with its gala week and the yacht races. My kids enjoy the river too, but it is the nature of football that I could be here today and gone tomorrow. If that came to pass, I would certainly miss Dundee and the club.'

Dundonians work hard and play hard and the generosity they extend to strangers is a tribute to the city's ability and determination to overcome adversity. Dundee's working women, tenacious in defending their rights, independent of spirit and resourceful in providing for their families, have been the beating heart of the community ever since they first flocked into the jute mills in their thousands. All too often they were the bread-winners when mass unemployment relegated Dundee's male workers to the status of 'kettle-boilers'. They were also a formidable political force in their own right. When the women of Dundee took exception to the city's brothels in the last century, they burnt them down. When mill owners cut wages, they went on strike and took to the streets. When denied the vote, they fuelled the suffragette movement. When their families were threatened by the curse of alcoholism, they organised in support of the temperance movement and succeeded in electing a prohibitionist MP.

In recent years women have been elected to Dundee district council in greater numbers and the council has a woman leader but, curiously, there are still relatively few women in the city's

The Hilltown clock, Dundee

Margaret Grant OBE

public life. An exception to the rule is Margaret Grant, who typifies the determination and understated courage of Dundee's womenfolk. Born in 1933 with what was then the virtually unknown condition of 'brittle bones', she received only three years' education and has suffered over 200 fractures in her lifetime. Yet, Margaret has overcome great hardship not just to marry, lead a normal life and bring up her daughter Yvonne, but also to found the national Brittle Bone Society which has brought practical help, understanding and hope to hundreds of brittle-bone children and their parents.

Her tireless efforts were recognised by her home town which named her a 'citizen of the year' and she was awarded the MBE in 1990. Despite the awards and recognition Margaret prefers to see herself as an ordinary Dundonian and is still campaigning for a better future for her fellow sufferers.

In the society's temporary home at Strathmartine Hospital, she recalls the early days: 'When I was a child there was really no understanding of the disease and I was told to drink lots of milk because I suffered from a calcium deficiency. I was given the wrong advice – they said that there was only a fifty-fifty chance of spreading the condition to any offspring. I spent five years of my life from the age of five in Maryfield Hospital and another three years in Stracathro Hospital. My father fought to get me an education and I was sent to Trefoil School in Edinburgh for three years. So I only really got three years of education and I still don't know where to put the commas.'

It was her housing difficulties and the problems of bringing up her daughter which prompted Margaret to form the charity. 'The society began in 1968 and was registered as a charity in 1972,' she explains. 'I started it after a social worker told me that there was no one to help someone like myself with brittle bones. We lived in a multistorey in a part of Dundee called Menzieshill then. Everyone used to say what a lovely view of the Tay I had but I could never see it because I was in a wheelchair. Living in a multi gave us a lot of headaches. My daughter Yvonne was in a wheelchair and she was too wee to reach the buttons in the lift. Also, we could not get both of our wheelchairs into the lift at the same time. Things were so backward, there was just so little help available. Eventually we got a council house near the Law and the Health and Welfare put ramps in. The trouble was that I had been given an adapted car by the Welfare on the understanding that it would be garaged. So we had to build a garage and nobody would help.

'I was really hurt that there was nothing being done for people with brittle bones and other similar conditions. So I started the society because I did not want anyone to feel how we felt. Things came to a head when my husband David went on short-time working in the jute mill and we couldn't keep up the payments on the garage. We eventually got a stay of execution and there was a piece in the *Sunday Mail* telling our story and saying that Margaret Grant wanted to start a club for people with brittle bones. Up until then I had only known two other people with the same condition.'

The publicity prompted a dozen people to get in touch with Margaret and since then the society has continued to grow, although it faces a constant strain on resources. It employs an occupational therapist based in London who travels around the country to treat an estimated 3,000 sufferers. Funds are raised to buy specialist wheelchairs, toys and sheepskins for children and babies. For dozens of children Margaret has become a second mother, advising parents how to wash, dress and cope with their babies.

Margaret is as proud of her home town as it is of her. 'I think Dundee is a good city and the folk are couthy,' she says. 'Without their support the society could not have kept going and a lot of poor people have helped us. I love Dundee and the Tay, I love to go to Broughty Ferry where I can share my anger or tranquillity with the river and take strength from the waves. For all of the awards that I have received, I am just a Dundee buddie.'

Chapter III

FIRTH OF TAY

Of all of Dundee's splendid vistas of the Tay, the view of Invergowrie Bay from the slopes of Balgay Hill is unsurpassed. The broad brackish waters of the river lazily balloon out over a huge basin, hemmed in by the Ochils to the south and the braes rising from the fertile Carse of Gowrie to the north. It is an impressive sight by any standards and, during the brief winter sunsets of November and December, the bay takes on a spectacular appearance when a sinking sun sets the sky ablaze.

With the construction of decent roads linking Dundee and Perth delayed until the early part of the nineteenth century, this stretch of the river formerly provided the main means of communication between the two cities. Sailing barges and steam paddlers jostled with their rivals to gain access to the narrow navigation channels between sandbanks with curious names like Haggis, Eppie's Taes, Durward's Scalp, Sure as Death, Carthagena, The Turk and Newfoundland Bank.

River trade was busy throughout the last century, particularly in the early part before the coming of the railways. The remains of the little ports which dotted both sides of the Tay and provided staging points for ferries and piers for the moving of grain, potatoes and stone, can still be seen. The Carse was served by the ports of Kingoodie, Cairnie Pier, Inchyra, Port Allen and Powgavie, which were established at the mouths of drainage ditches or 'pows' where they joined the river.

On the south bank Fife, too, had its ports. A deepwater channel was dredged through mudflats to the hamlet of Balmerino, and a more substantial harbour was established at Newburgh which remained busy with an international trade to the continent right up to the 1970s. A ferry crossing operated up to the turn of the century at Ferryfield of Carpow where the Earn joins the Tay and where the Romans are believed to have built a pontoon crossing across the river in AD 80.

The ferry boatmen and sailors on the trading barques have long gone but, as the river narrows, it continues to provide employment and recreation for local people. Salmon-netters can be seen hauling in their nets in great arcs on to the beaches of the river at Kinfauns. And, just as the salmon-netting begins each spring, others are drawing their annual harvest of Britain's biggest reed-bed at Errol to a close. Using 'moon buggies' with giant amphibious wheels, they cut beds of reeds which extend to seven miles long on the north bank of the river

The steamer Cleopatra *plied between Perth and Dundee*

between Errol and Inchture and send the Tay reeds south to meet an insatiable demand for thatch in a conservation-minded England.

Wildfowlers haunt the river-bank and ever-hopeful anglers try their luck as the Tay, still tidal up to Perth, takes on the familiar characteristics of river rather than estuary. And, at Newburgh, the last of the Tay's sparling-fishers still plies his trade pursuing a tiny cucumber-scented cousin of the salmon which was once one of Europe's culinary delicacies.

Both banks of the river are rich in opportunities for exploration and enjoyment. The Carse villages of Invergowrie, Liff, Fowlis, Longforgan, Inchture, Abernyte, Errol, Rait and Kinfauns are not just dormitory villages for their city neighbours. Like their counterparts across the river – Balmerino, Newburgh and Abernethy which climb up the north-facing slopes of the Ochils – they are working villages with their own sense of identity and community.

Among those to make their home in the Carse is international bestselling author Rosamunde Pilcher, who exchanged her native Cornwall for Dundee when she married a member of the jute-manufacturing Cox family. In 1956 she and her husband Graham sought out the tranquillity of the countryside around Invergowrie and moved into the house they had built for themselves at East Pilmore.

Rosamunde first began writing short stories for magazines as a teenager and has now achieved a scarcely imaginable success. Her career, which started as a hobby pursued from the kitchen table to earn pin money, triumphed in 1990 when *The Shell Seekers* knocked American literary giant Tom Wolfe out of the US number one bestseller slot by outselling his massively hyped *Bonfire of the Vanities*. *September* followed and Rosamunde is currently working on a third blockbuster.

Attaining celebrity status in her mid-60s is accepted with grace by this mother and grandmother. 'It was quite funny,' she recalls, 'hearing the news that the book had first entered the *New York Times* bestseller list. To get on to the list is a huge selling point, and when my publisher phoned from the States I could hear champagne corks popping. Yet here I was in Invergowrie!'

Enormous international sales of the book, in 20 different languages, led on to a television serialisation of *The Shell Seekers* starring Angela Lansbury, and to Rosamunde being voted 'author of the year' in Germany. Her belief that millions of readers longed for a good read set outwith the parameters of '*Dallas* and *Dynasty* and which did not concentrate on shopping and sex' proved correct, and now she quietly enjoys a fame which seems to touch her only rarely in her lovely Perthshire hideaway.

'People always ask me if I wished that success had come earlier, when I was younger. But I am just so grateful that it came at all. I have always lived a divided life between my writing and my ordinary life and never really talked about it. Quite a lot of people who knew me for years never actually knew that I wrote until *The Shell Seekers*. My family, of course, are delighted. After seeing me working all these years, I think that they are awfully pleased.

'I have been a very lucky woman. My husband, who was very badly wounded when he served in the Black Watch in Germany, has nonetheless had a full and active life. We have two sons and two daughters aged between 34 and 44 and I am a proud grandmother.

International bestseller Rosamunde Pilcher at home by the Tay

'I have been lucky too, to live in this area. I walk my dog down on the foreshore of the Tay near here and it is spectacular. The river never looks the same and there is always something to see, especially the geese and shell duck. The river adds to the quality of life here and I love it.'

In these days of telecommuting when it is possible to take the publishing world by storm from Invergowrie, the prospect of living in the Carse is an attractive one, and villages threatened by depopulation two or three decades ago are now thriving.

The clearest picture of recent social changes in these villages is presented by Abernyte where, in 1988, the good people of the parish produced *Abernyte – Portrait of a Perthshire Village*. Adhering to the format of the Statistical Accounts undertaken in 1792, 1837 and 1966, the villagers paint a picture of a vibrant community.

Nestling in the shadow of Dunsinane Hill, reputed site of Macbeth's castle, Abernyte and its surrounding area includes the picturesque village of Knapp with its converted water-mill, a scene immortalised by McIntosh Patrick, and, higher up, the old farm toun of Lochton. The area was, and still is, primarily agricultural. In its heyday a two-mile stretch of the Knapp Burn was said to have boasted the greatest concentration of mills in Scotland, with five corn mills, four lint mills, a barley mill and a threshing mill all supported by local farms. But few of today's residents work on the land and while the concept of the absentee landlord was nothing new to the hardy tenant farmers of 1792, none could have imagined in those far-off days that the largest landowner in the area would one day be the British Rail Pension Fund.

After decades of decline, the population in the parish has recovered to 266 although it remains short of the 1792 level of 350. Just under half of the residents were born in the area with almost a quarter coming in from England or abroad. Pressure on water and sewage services has put a welcome brake on housebuilding in Abernyte as in much of the Carse.

Those lucky enough to make their home in the area are usually only too well aware of their good fortune. Keith Brockie is a young Scottish artist who was brought up in Fife and attended art college in Dundee. From his home at Dron Farm, where a tributary of the Tay runs through the garden, he has carved out a successful career as a wildlife artist and his passion for the river inspired *The Silvery Tay*, his popular book of bird-life illustrations.

Keith's interest in wildlife has led to his involvement in conservation work in the Tay valley area and he is one of those fortunate but not uncommon Taysiders to combine his interests with his work. 'The two influences in my life have been art and wildlife which have converged quite successfully over the years,' he recounts. 'The landscape of the Tay is particularly unique and is rich in wildlife, providing an artist like myself with countless subjects. I am constantly amazed at the diversity of birds and animals in this area and I am lucky to live near a river which has a variety of wildlife ranging from seals to waders.'

Appreciative of a lifestyle which allows him the satisfaction of earning a living from his hobby, Keith is repaying nature by his work with bird-ringing groups and with the dedicated ornithologists who have encouraged the return and growth of the osprey population in Tayside.

'The ringing group monitors sandmartins and herons,' he says. 'It is a nice way to handle birds and allows me a total involvement with the subjects I am painting. Our work with ospreys is beginning to pay off; there are now more than ten pairs in the Tayside area. Sadly, two or three nests do get robbed each year. Recently we were helped by the Royal Marines who mounted a guard over some nests and we put razor wire on trees with nests to deter thieves.'

The biggest factor in the successful return of the ospreys, Keith stresses, has been the relatively unspoiled nature of much of the Tay itself. 'The birds have spread throughout Tayside because of the river and its lochs which provide them with plentiful amounts of food. Being so unspoiled, the Tay gives the birds a chance to survive and there is room for many more pairs.

'The Tay is one of Britain's luckiest rivers because its surrounding area has not been so intensively industrialised as many others. The vast numbers of eider duck which breed on the river are indicative of its healthy state but I fear that, in the years to come, increasing forestry will do damage to the biological life-cycle of the river. If fish-spawning areas are damaged there will be a definite knock-on effect.'

The braes of the Carse are mercifully unwooded and their remarkable beauty encourages frequent comparisons with scenic parts of the Rhine valley. In place of grapevines, raspberry canes climb up the south-facing slopes and, in imitation of teutonic ruins, Victorian aristocrats constructed follies on the hilltops of Kinnoul and Kinfauns as reminders of their 'grand tour'.

Through the trees visitors can catch a glimpse of the mansion houses and castles which testify to the huge wealth accrued from the agricultural improvement of the Carse with its fertile but heavy soil of clays and silts deposited by the river over the centuries. The ruined House of Gray hints at former opulence while the neighbouring magnificence of Rossie Priory, the former seat of the Kinnaird family, is now a luxury private home leased to a cousin of Princess Diana. Nearby, Castle Huntly, formerly a fortress of the Strathmore family, provides less commodious accommodation as a young offenders' institution.

Fingask Castle, Errol Park House, Kinfauns Castle, Seggieden House, Megginch Castle, Glencarse House, Pitfour Castle, Glendoick House and Kinnaird Castle are among the astonishing number of great houses crammed into the 40 square miles that make up the Carse of Gowrie. These houses are memorials to the economic power which came from agriculture, but across the river, on the south bank, Abernethy's historic round tower, the strongholds of Ballinbreich and Elcho Castles, and the ruins of Balmerino Abbey and Lindores Abbey are reminders of the area's earlier political significance when, up to the twelfth century, Scone was the symbolic heart of Scotland and the Scottish kings spent much of their time on the banks of the Tay.

From the eighteenth century, the 'big house' with a small village of peasantry at its gates was the classic Carse layout. Errol Park House with the village of Errol, 'the capital of the Carse', just outside the estate's perimeter wall typified this 'rich man in his castle, poor man at his gate' approach to town-planning.

The feudal power of the Hay family, the original Earls of Errol, has waned since the family was first ennobled by Kenneth, King of the Scots. Grateful for assistance in beating off an invasion by the Danes, he awarded the Hays all the land between the points where his falcon landed and, in the process, bequeathed the Carse one of its most colourful folk stories commemorated by the Hawk's Stane at the village of St Madoes.

The village of Errol as it stands today is a perfect candidate for the radio programme *Down Your Way*. The historic lack of stone around the village led to a still thriving brick-making industry with buildings of the original odd-sized Errol brick still to be discovered in the area. The reed harvesters have set up headquarters on the old Second World War aerodrome, along with a parachute club and a race track for horse and trap driving. The former Errol Railway Station has been splendidly refurbished by volunteers and the village's former smiddy converted into a cosy restaurant.

Sunset over the Kinnoul Hill

Janet McOuat, with the Hawk's Stane in her garden at St Madoes

Opposite Errol on the south bank is the ancient and curious Royal Burgh of Newburgh. Although slightly tatty and down-at-heel, Newburgh is a gem of a village, somewhat reminiscent in its architecture, which tumbles down to meet the river, of the East Neuk of Fife. It is a hamlet just waiting for gentrification and, with low property prices and improved road networks to Glasgow and Edinburgh, that prospect cannot be far away.

Once prosperous with a busy harbour, textile industry and linoleum factory, Newburgh went into decline in the late 1960s and is now largely a commuter centre. But it has a distinctive charm and identity with Georgian-style architecture in the High Street and glorious views of the river.

Salmon-netting once employed scores of local men and each summer until the 1960s attracted dozens of casually employed salmon-netters from the Western Isles. Few of the once numerous salmon stations are still in use and the number of fish has declined sharply since local man Tom Jarvis first started netting with his father more than 40 years ago. 'Catches have gone down dramatically in the last few years. You were really born to the salmon fishing. The season runs from February to August and much depends on where and when you fish. There were hundreds of salmon stations up and down the river and we even fished from cairns built up on the river-bed opposite Newburgh, behind Mugdrum and near Cairnie Pier,' says Tom.

'They use motor cobles now but, when I was young, we had to row. It was quite hazardous, being out in the river at night to catch the tide. If a wind came down from the Earn valley you could easily lose a boat. We used to make all our nets. They were hand-knitted and there are still people locally who have the skill.

'The salmon-netting was hard work but I suppose my worst experiences were during the war. As a youngster I would help my father and often we would get bodies in the nets. It was pretty frightening when you were out at night with only the eerie light of storm lanterns.'

The Tay's vast network of tributaries makes it a natural salmon river and offers the king of fish dozens, perhaps hundreds, of spawning grounds. But netting at sea by the Faroese, Icelanders and English using drift-nets banned in Scottish waters, has been just one of the factors causing the decimation of salmon numbers. Tom expresses sadness at the decline in salmon runs and the effect on employment: 'There is only a fraction now of the stations that once were here. And where a station employed six or seven men, it has been reduced to four or five.'

Nonetheless, salmon-netting still provides some welcome seasonal employment for both locals and students. For one of the latter the experience of working the nets led to a passionate interest in the subject of Tay salmon fishing. Iain Robertson, now a lecturer at Perth College of Further Education, completed a thesis on 'Tay Salmon Fisheries in the Nineteenth Century' and is an authority on the subject: 'Salmon fishing on the Tay was important seasonal work running from December or February until August. As the season progressed the numbers would build up to around 400 people, many of them weavers from Newburgh. Most of the fishermen worked part-time apart, that is, from the salmon merchants known as salmon taxmen who rented the fishings out and engaged the crews.'

Some of these 'taxmen', most notably John Richardson who, in 1781, built Pitfour Castle at St Madoes, became extremely rich from the salmon trade. But relatively little of the wealth harvested from the river was invested in Tayside, and the main economic spin-off of the fishing was limited boat-building and net-making.

Hauling salmon nets, February 1949

Two, and even three hundred years ago the wealthy of London, Paris and Genoa dined on Tay salmon. 'Up until the eighteenth century only "raw" salmon could be sent to London, which was the principal market, and then only in the winter', says Iain. 'The fish were packed in boxes with straw as insulation but after March the weather was too warm for this method. Later the fish began to be salted and a large export trade in salted salmon developed. There was little demand for this type of fish in Britain but it was popular in the Catholic countries of Europe and there are records of Newburgh boats taking salted salmon to Genoa.

'In the mid-eighteenth century a new preservation method called "kitting" – named after the little barrels called "kits" – was introduced. This involved parboiling the salmon and packing them in vinegar and was a product which found a ready market in Britain. Later, the introduction of ice improved the quality of the fish and made salmon a luxury that was in great demand. Ice stations were built on the river, at Balmerino, Perth and Seggie Den, for instance, which comprised of a storage hut and a pond from which ice was taken in the winter.'

The salmon taxmen were eventually bought out in 1899 when the Tay Salmon Fishing Company was formed, but even before then they did not always have things their own way. According to Iain, 'There was definitely a poaching industry around Newburgh where the law was very ineffective until the 1820s. Poaching then had a resurgence when the railways started. The poachers used drift-nets and forced merchants to buy from them on pain of having

Salmon netters at a Tay bothy, 1870

their boats smashed and nets torn. It was quite violent at times and some people were killed. Matters came to a head in the Battle of Gutter Hole near Newburgh where two fishermen drowned during a skirmish.'

Among the salmon merchants' most bitter rivals were the sparling-fishers who were after another fish but often found salmon in their nets. Teeming shoals of sparling – a silver-green and yellow fish, oddly smelling of cucumber and growing up to 14 inches in length – once sustained a booming industry, cashing in on the de-luxe status of a fish still sought-after in France but virtually ignored in Scotland. From the turn of the century to the Second World War the special trains which took the salmon to the London market carried another, equally prized delicacy. Tay sparling packed in ice commanded top prices among restaurateurs who favoured its light, delicate white flesh.

The waters of the Tay between the rail bridge and the river's confluence with the Earn are alive with sparling. One of the most memorable scenes of the river in early spring is provided by the aeronautic displays of cormorants which leave their roosts on the rail bridge to gorge on the silvery shoals.

Pollution has killed off the sparling population of the Forth and only the Tay and the Solway now sustain a fish which has gone out of fashion. Britain's last professional sparling fisherman is Newburgh resident Charlie Johnston. Now semi-retired, he is passing his skills on to younger enthusiasts. 'The sparling spend all of their lives in brackish water. They spawn in fresh water and go down towards the sea to grow before returning upstream to spawn again. They very rarely go further than the rail bridge, although when we fished for sprats in the estuary the odd one would be caught. We knew right away, as soon as the net came out of the water, if there was a sparling in amongst the sprats. You smelled the cucumber even if there was only one fish among two cran of sprats. The fish at the rail bridge tend to be green-backed, the colour changing to yellow-gold as they go upstream.

'Very few people know about the sparling,' continues Charlie. 'I once took some to Anstruther, which is only 25 miles away, and showed them to fishermen there. They didn't have a clue what they were. Sparlings were a luxury fish. At the turn of the century a box 12 inches wide and just one fish deep would fetch nearly half-a-crown in London. After the last war, I remember a fleet of Dutch fishermen sailing specially to the Tay for the sparling fishing.'

Sparling yawls would lower their nets on booms into the water just before the tide ebbed or turned, letting the action of the water push the fish into the nets. The best results are in the muddy waters of the Tay near the mouth of the Earn, which can make hauling in the nets arduous and dirty work.

'Sparling still sells in Liverpool and Plymouth,' says Charlie. 'When we tried it in Perth, it sold well to the Chinese community. But I doubt if it will become popular in Scotland again. They were best shallow-fried in oatmeal, just like herring, and I think that the shortage of fat and oil during the war really killed demand for the fish. Bigger vessels and increased traffic on the river would also make fishing more difficult. But I would like to think that we could keep the tradition alive and I am showing a young lad in Newburgh how it's done.'

Like fishing, agriculture now employs far fewer workers, but only because of the success of modern farming methods. Agriculture remains a vital economic activity along the entire length of the Tay but if any area can lay claim to the title of 'Garden of Scotland', it is surely the Carse of Gowrie.

Once famed for its orchards, the remnants of which explode in clouds of white blossom in May and June, the produce of the Carse was exported as far as London in the eighteenth century when the street-seller's cry of 'apples from the top of the trees of Monorgan!' rang out in the capital to encourage buyers. The area's apple-growing expertise went further afield when two local brothers emigrated to New Zealand in the last century and, noting the similarities to Scotland, introduced the orchard to that part of the Antipodes.

Today soft fruit has displaced the orchards and dreels of raspberry canes hug the braes of the Carse while, on gentler slopes, strawberries, gooseberries and blackcurrants are grown. Fittingly for an area which saw the invention of an early form of reaper by local man Patrick Bell in 1827, the 'Fair Land of Gowrie' is host to the pioneering Scottish Crop Research Institute at Mylnefield. Among the 400 people employed at the Invergowrie base are some of Britain's most eminent botanists, quietly working on developing new varieties of raspberry and blackcurrant and combatting pests and diseases to potatoes, brassicas and root vegetables.

Although the SCRI enjoys an international reputation in its field, it has until quite recently kept its light under a bushel as far as the general public is concerned. Its best-known achievement, but far from its most important, is the development of the Tayberry, a large, blue-black, succulent hybrid of the raspberry and blackberry. The Tay valley constitutes Western Europe's largest raspberry-growing belt and it was the inter-war failure of this crop,

Sampling Tayberries at the Scottish Crop Research Institute

Thousands of Taysiders still go berry-picking

originally popularised in the area by a Blairgowrie lawyer, which led to the eventual establishment of the SCRI.

As Dr Derek Perry, scientific liaison officer at Mylnefield, explains, 'In the 1930s the large raspberry crop in Tayside began to fail. Yields were down, leaves curled up and the berries were not so large and juicy. In the late 1940s a raspberry investigation unit headed by Dr Conway Wood and Dr Colin Cadman was established. The Scottish Department of Agriculture bought Mylnefield in 1951 and the SCRI grew out of these beginnings.'

Cadman and Wood became authorities on viral diseases caused by aphids and microscopic worms. They went on to develop methods of chemical control and new disease-resistant varieties, The SCRI acquired international recognition for research in these areas and scientists now travel from all over the world to study at its microbiology section.

The SCRI developed new strains of raspberry with their Glen Clova, released in the 1970s, now accounting for three-quarters of the raspberries grown in Tayside. It was followed with the Glen Prosen and Glen Moy varieties and a new range of hardy blackcurrants named after Scottish mountains: Ben Nevis, Ben Lomond, Ben Sarek and Ben Alder. Potatoes are now the most important aspect of the SCRI's work. Tayside is the main source of seed potatoes in Britain and the SCRI research is vital in Scotland's bid to increase exports to Mediterranean countries.

But it is the fruit named after the River Tay which has provided the public with the most enduring example of the institute's work. 'The development of the Tayberry was initially a curiosity,' reveals Dr Perry 'The breeding programme for berries produced interesting crosses, among them the Loganberry. The Tayberry was produced by Derek Jennings, who had earlier developed the Glen Clova raspberry. A cross between the raspberry and the blackberry, the Tayberry is a large berry which tastes of both. It has not been universally popular with plantation people as they are accustomed to marketing raspberries. Nor is it as easy to process. Unlike the raspberry, the plug in the berry tends to stay in which makes jam-making difficult. But it has been popular among gardeners and horticulturalists who are attracted by its size.'

Despite the efforts of the Invergowrie scientists, however, farmers along the Tay have suffered at the hands of politicians and subsidised competitors. The SCRI has conquered the curse of raspberry viruses but is powerless in the face of cheap Eastern European imports which are steadily reducing the raspberry acreage in Perthshire and Angus. Farmers are putting up a spirited defence to protect an industry which provides seasonal employment to an estimated 40,000 pickers and processors during the rush to harvest the fruit in July and August. For many of these workers, unemployed and picked up in dilapidated buses that tour the bleak council housing schemes of Perth and Dundee, 'the berries' are an annual lifeline. Providing they successfully dodge the social security inspectors who follow the 'berry buses' as they drop off the pickers, vital extra cash can be used to buy the necessities of life.

The camps and 'tin cities' of corrugated iron which accommodated thousands of pickers from the West of Scotland in the 1930s, '40s and '50s are long gone. A few hundred still make their annual pilgrimage for a two-week working holiday in the countryside. Their ranks are now swollen with new recruits from the former Eastern Bloc countries, young students eager to earn hard currency. For several years Andrew Bain has employed Czech and East German students at his farm at Flocklones, just up the hill from Mylnefield. His farm – with a canteen, toilets and showers for the pickers – is a far cry from the primitive conditions which still prevail on some farms.

'Most Dundee pickers are still conditioned to picking for the pulp-processing market but that has all changed now,' says Andrew, 'We have to pick a fresh quality product for the supermarket trade and the Eastern Europeans don't have to be taught to change old habits.'

Lack of pickers, once cited as a major difficulty, is no longer a problem, but Andrew Bain can list many more. Like many fruit farmers he is at a crossroads about whether to continue with his 23 acres of raspberries and strawberries. Even allowing for the traditional predisposition of farmers to complain of the weather and bearing in mind the old Carse adage, 'You never see a farmer on a bike', the financial crisis facing the fruit farmer is real and serious.

The influx of cheap, subsidised Polish, Hungarian and Yugoslav raspberries in the 1980s knocked the bottom out of the pulp-processing market, persuading Tayside farmers to plough in almost half of the region's raspberry acreage. A ban on the spraying of Dinoseb, a growth inhibitor which reduced the foliage concealing berries, because of its allegedly harmful side-effects, was a further blow.

For Andrew, however, it is the farmer's old adversary, the weather, which has become the biggest problem. 'The changes in the climate are really worrying and I don't think that the general public realise just how much the weather is changing,' he says. 'Lack of winters mean that weeds can continue to grow and pests can continue to multiply. But worse than that, lack of snow means that the ground is very dry. There is no body in it. We had a drought year in 1984 and it was really hot, but the winter's snow had topped up the land with water and we had a fine crop. This year we had 90 days without rain and when it did rain we ended up with a flash flood and the top soil washed out of the fields.

'It is pretty tough when you are depending on the weather to make a living. The prices for our products are dropping but our costs and overheads are rising. I really don't know where we go from here.'

Andrew is not the first farmer on the banks of the Tay to issue that particular *cri de coeur*. Diversification has become all the rage as farmers reap a bitter harvest for their efforts. At East Inchmichael farm, near Errol, Ron Gillies and Judith Findlay have turned their attention from farming to wine production. Bolstering frequent comparisons of this part of the Tay valley with the scenery of the Rhine, the couple produce and sell 30,000 bottles of wine annually and have built up a strong local following in Tayside and Fife.

With a heady alcoholic strength of 14 per cent, the wine lives up to its Cairn o' Mhor label and if the name suggests a sense of fun, wine-making is nonetheless a serious £100,000-a-year business down on the farm.

'We make six different wines here,' says Ron. 'They are all produced from local fruit. Our strawberry wine is a sweet rosé, the raspberry a fruity red and the elderberry a full-bodied red. We also make a bramble wine which is a drier red and goes very well with meat and game dishes. Our two whites are made from oak leaves and we have perfected a dry and a sweeter variety.'

Judith gave up a medical career for the good life in the Carse and has few regrets: 'During the summer we will pick a ton of elderberries and a third of a ton of brambles. It can be hard work. But on a nice summer day, with the sun shining and the birds singing, your worries vanish.

'We grow our own rasps, strawberries and brambles here and, to the horror of local people, we are planting elder bushes which are regarded by many as a weed,' she laughs. 'We intend to try producing elderflower cordial. We made a trial batch last year and it was really nice.'

Ron Gillies and Judith Findlay at Cairn O'Mhor Winery

As wine-making becomes more business-like and efficient at the farm, Ron and Judith are finding that the long hours once necessary are beginning to shorten. 'It is better than farming and more profitable,' concludes Judith.

Jim Somers would be among the first to echo Judith's sentiments. After years of gruelling hard work running his market garden on the flat banks of the Tay at Walnut Grove, beneath the steep escarpment of Kinnoul Hill, Jim gave up market gardening to establish a Heavy Horse Centre which, since opening in 1987, has become a popular tourist attraction.

Like most farming folk, Jim did not find the move easy but as he bluntly admits, 'The growing of fruit and vegetables was proving such a shambles that I had to do something else or go under. I had always kept horses on my farm and visitors would come to the farmhouse asking for a look at the Clydesdales. Often, at the end of a day in the fields, I had to face a cold tea after showing tourists the one thing about the farm that I really loved – the horses. So, I eventually decided to go for it and open the Heavy Horse Centre. The farmland was grassed over and we started to build stables and the basics for a visitor centre.'

The ploughman's skill at the Heavy Horse Centre

Ian and Roy Miller at Jamesfield Organic Farm

Organic farming may sound new-fangled and vaguely trendy to many, but not to 'fly Fifers'. On the slopes of the Ochils above Newburgh, on Wester Clunie farm, Jack Lawrie has proved the old saying of 'where there's muck there's money' with the help, that is, of 20,000 Californian Red Worms.

Wester Clunie has become the first commercial producer of organic compost in Scotland. Jack dreamt up the idea to supplement his income from the 160-acre mixed arable farm and is now producing hundreds of tonnes of organic compost for sale to the English market and local garden centres. 'The economic future of farmers like myself is very much in the balance, so I was looking for something new that would not upset our method of farming and which required minimum capital investment.'

Since then, the Californian Reds have done their work, munching through tonnes of manure to produce non-chemical, smell-free compost. And Jack has mastered the art of worm-keeping. 'Every month or so the worms are fed a six-inch layer of manure, which they work their way up through, eating it all the time,' he reveals. 'They digest and break down the manure, getting rid of all the straw and leaving a rich worm-cast, increasing the nutrition of the manure by 100 per cent.

'Care must be taken looking after the worms,' Jack emphasises, 'You must ensure that the manure is kept at the correct level. Temperature and moisture also affect the worms. In the winter they are much less active. They are always working their way upwards through the layers, and if you gave them too little they would vanish. At harvest time the worms are removed and the compost is left to dry naturally.'

The mysteries of the Californian Red are secrets that Jack may care to share with his neighbours at Jamesfield farm where, by coincidence, the entire 300-acre farm has been turned over to organic methods. Jamesfield went organic in 1986 and brothers Ian and Roy Miller are now reaping the rewards of a difficult five-year conversion period. Ian stresses that the decision to go organic was 'ethical rather then financial' and that part of the farm has been let to the Scottish Agricultural College for the assessment of different natural growing methods.

'I think that in their heart of hearts, most farmers know that it cannot be right to continue applying more and more chemicals to the land,' says Ian. 'But sadly, it seems it will take some kind of a crisis before people change.'

The farm has been in the family for over 50 years, and it was the chance discovery that a six-acre cow pasture had been left completely untouched by chemicals since 1939 which encouraged the brothers to try organic farming. Today, root vegetables, brassicas, cereals and lettuce are grown the natural way and Ian reports that margins are much better than on conventionally grown produce. But things have not been easy.

'The conversion period is difficult because when chemicals and fertilisers are withdrawn the fertility of the soil intially drops dramatically. There is little produce to sell and virtually no premium,' recalls Ian painfully. 'If you didn't have the sacrifices at the beginning it would be very viable. It takes about five years before you see any big improvement in yield and then the margins start improving.'

Demand for organic produce is soaring in the health-conscious 1990s and the Miller brothers have found a ready market for their produce. 'Ethically, it has been well worth it,' concludes Ian, 'But it will take time to bear fruit financially.'

Like farmers the world over, Ian feels a special attachment to his native soil and, in common with most who live by the river, he feels privileged to live in beautiful surroundings which are relatively unspoilt. 'Our farm is right on the river,' he says proudly. 'And our land includes 30 acres of reed-bed which has been declared a Site of Special Scientific Interest because of the rare plants and wildlife.'

Opposite the reed beds at Jamesfield lies one of the Tay's few islands. Itself swathed in reeds, Mugdrum Island has, for its size, an impressive history. The remains of what must have been an imposing Roman fortress at Carpow are close by and the island is thought to have been the central span for a pontoon bridge constructed by Agricola's invaders. The island was home, too, for the Picts who left behind their familiar calling cards carved in stone. Even earlier, iron-age residents built a fort on the islet.

Deserted now, Mugdrum Island was farmed up to the 1920s and its survival is largely due to the labours of Napoleonic prisoners of war who provided so many of Scotland's great landowners with slave labour to complete ambitious civil engineering projects. For these poor souls, Mugdrum Island must have been more like Devil's Island, as they toiled up to their waists in water to build a dyke around the island and undertake land reclamation work.

Mugdrum, named after St Macgidrim, a mysterious ancient monk, appears to float freely in the river and has lost none of its ability to entrance visitors. Such are its powers of inspiration that one local artist, Derek Robertson, has been moved to produce and privately publish a lavishly illustrated volume, *The Mugdrum*, in just 50 copies.

'The book grew out of my fascination with Mugdrum Island and its historical associations,' explains Derek. 'I was born in Fife and explored Mugdrum as a kid. The fascination of the place to me is the mix of historical fact and mystical elements.

'Although uninhabited today, cattle graze on the island during the summer and enter the island via a type of entrance gate through the dyke built in the 1790s. There is also a huge wall on the island used to keep out high tides. I talked to the last man who was born and lived on Mugdrum. He said that when the gate in the high tide wall was inadvertently left open, horses would be up to their bellies in water in the middle of the island.'

The reeds which wreath Mugdrum have colonised both sides of the Tay. Originally planted by landowners to protect reclaimed land, they have grown into Britain's greatest reed beds and for some they provide a living. For 20 years Graham Craig has harvested the reeds and he recently mortgaged his home to establish Tayreed, a company which provides full-time employment for three people. Well over 100,000 bunches are harvested each year for the English market. From December to March, Graham and his men cut the reeds in difficult conditions and then spend the rest of the year cleaning, processing and batching the thatch.

'We finish cutting the reeds by mid-April', he says. 'That is partly because the quality of the reeds is better during the winter, but mainly because on this part of the Tay there are many birds which rely on the beds. We work closely with the Tay area bird-ringing group, and their surveys have shown that there is much higher bird-nesting in areas that have been harvested.

'Harvesting also improves the quality of the reeds, which get better with each year. On average, we will cut around 130,000 bunches annually and, weighing in at 8 to 10lb in a bunch, that is a heck of a lot of reeds.'

Reed-cutting is demanding and unpleasant work with the air often thick with choking dust. Tayreed supplies around a tenth of the British market, fighting off competition from Poland and Hungary by undercutting them on prices.

And Graham is proud of his product: 'A thatched roof of wheat reed will last only 15 or 20 years whereas reeds taken from river-beds will last up to 80 years. The insulation value and natural benefit that is acquired mean that a thatched roof is extraordinarily environment-friendly. Most people who have their houses thatched receive grant aid, and when you compare the cost of thatch to slates and tiles, at around £5,000 for an average house, it is not that much more expensive.'

The conservationists are not the only enthusiasts with whom Graham has to share his wilderness. Wildfowling, once a hugely popular sport which spawned clubs in Dundee factories and local groups in the villages of the Carse, is now the pastime of only a few hunters who lurk in the ditches and pows that empty into the Tay. But what they lack in numbers is made up for in dedication.

Alan Moncur is the acknowledged crackshot of the Carse. A wildfowler for over 30 years, his colleagues readily defer to his tightly guarded knowledge of the river and its banks near his Invergowrie home.

Harvesting the reed beds, Errol

A tantalising glimpse of the Tay

'The best time for going wildfowling is from September to the end of February,' he reveals. 'At that time the ducks and geese gather in large numbers waiting to migrate and there is a vast amount of birds sitting in the reed beds from Invergowrie up to Errol, which is my favourite patrol.

'You get yourself into a good position so that you can see the birds coming over. A lot of people go on to the sandbanks but that's a method I just don't believe in. The number of birds you can shoot varies according to planning, luck, weather and the time of day. The best times and places are found out through trial and error over many, many years.'

Alan stresses the levels of skill, patience, discomfort and local knowledge required as factors in the decline of the sport. But conservation measures introduced to prevent the sale of slaughtered geese have played an important part in the diminishing popularity of wildfowling on the Tay.

Hamish McAlpine, for one, is sad to see the decline of wildfowling. Best known as the popular goalkeeper for Dundee United, Hamish is more accustomed to saving shots than taking them but talks about hunting on the Tay with real enthusiasm.

'Local knowledge of the river and the area is vital if wildfowling is to be safe and successful. You can take up a shooting position on the sandbanks, but you have to be very wary of the tides. Also, you have to be careful what you're walking on and how far out you are. It is a sport with an apprenticeship phase, and knowledge can only be built up over a number of years. I lived in Invergowrie and was ideally placed to learn the trade of wildfowling. Even so, it took ages of watching the ducks and geese to find the right positions at the right times.

'The best places to go were all along the foreshore from Invergowrie to Errol. There were unwritten rules that local groups would keep to their own territory. There was a Newburgh lot, an Errol lot and groups right along the length of the river.'

As Hamish recalls, however, there was a phase when wildfowling became too popular. 'At times, when wildfowling attracted big numbers, there was bad shooting. The constant hammering at the birds meant the whole area would be disturbed. And the birds aren't daft. They would disappear somewhere else until it all calmed down. Sometimes the amount of wildfowling was ridiculous. Town folk with duck calls and all that nonsense. Some of them would wander along smoking cigars – as if the birds couldn't see or something!'

'The law states that wild geese cannot be sold and that has stopped the massive slaughter of the birds, but there are still those who net the birds on the ground. These people have no interest in the birds or the countryside; they are just out for sheer bloody profit. I just went shooting for the pleasure of it and one of the biggest pleasures was watching the weather change around the river. The light moves in beautiful ways across the length of the river and at times when you have to sit through the night, Dundee is an impressive sight at dawn with the streetlamps twinkling and the city bathed in soft light.'

Many treasure this stretch of the river for the livelihood and the leisure opportunities it offers but for many more it is quite simply the lifestyle which is unbeatable. It was a key factor in persuading Anne and Derek Brow to give up a high-flying life in Hong Kong. The couple set up home in the Carse village of St Madoes and have established a successful cheese-making business in nearby Perth. Anne is emphatic that their move has been the right one: 'The quality of life here is unrivalled. The beauty of the Tay and the surrounding countryside is an inspiration to us. We often take walks by the river and the countryside provides us with a wealth of natural flavouring additives which we use in our recipes. The lush grass of the Carse of Gowrie is ideal for our purposes.'

The Brows' traditional cheeses are made to Orkney recipes Anne collected from her grandmother. 'Traditional cheeses are really like a fine wine and the land around the Tay provides soil and plants which ensure that the finished product is of extremely high quality, with a rich variety of flavours from the local milk. Many local folk have said to us that they haven't tasted cheese like ours since their granny was alive, so I'm pretty sure that there is a similarity between the old Perthshire cheeses and our Orkney varieties.'

The Brows started their business in the late 1980s and are now exporting to Germany from their enlarged premises. The Carse has inspired Anne to create an entirely new cheese: 'There was a community of monks at St Madoes and I am sure that they made cheese here. Wherever there were monks there was always an abundance of honey and dairy products. It gave me the idea of doing a "Maddoch" cheese. We dust the rind with cinders and the contrast of the stark white cheese and dark rind has proved very popular.

'The Tay has always supported the people who live by its banks and I wouldn't dream of living anywhere else.'

Perth Museum

Chapter IV

PERTH:
THE PEARL OF THE TAY

As the Tay narrows and turns northwards, its tidal waters meet the clear fresh torrent drained from 3,000 square miles of fertile fields and Highland hills. Here, where the River Almond joins the rush to the sea, lies Perth – the Pearl of the Tay.

Seemingly impervious to the weary grind of recession and depression, Perth has emerged over the last decade as a confident commercial and tourism centre, strong in identity and sure in purpose. Not for Perth the fading dowdiness of a tweedy county town which loomed so large less than 20 years ago. The Fair City has built on its strengths and avoided resting on its laurels.

The contrast with Perth's larger neighbour to the east could not be more striking. In the Tay's tale of two cities the gap between prospering Perth and struggling Dundee seems destined to widen: where Dundee has yet to succeed, Perth has triumphed; while Dundee's population declines, Perth's rises; and while Dundee wrestles with its apparently intractable identity crisis, Perth gets down to business, emerging as an attractive location for corporate headquarters.

A significant element of Perth's easy self-confidence and prosperity derives from its strong sense of identity and purpose. Always a strategic crossroads, Perth was Scotland's ancient capital until 1482 when James III transferred the seat of government to Edinburgh. Its location at the mouth of the Tay valley made it a natural gateway to the Highlands, a factor recognised as early as AD 80 when the Romans, led by Agricola, built a fort at a crossing place near the Tay's confluence with the Almond and named it Bertha – from which the city takes its modern name. The next wave of newcomers were the Celtic missionaries from Iona who travelled up the Tay to spread the word of Columba's gospel.

Perth subsequently developed as an important religious centre and was known as St John's Toun after its church of that name was established in 1126. Monasteries and religious orders of various persuasions flourished. For centuries Perth was pivotal in Scottish affairs, both political and ecclesiastical. When Scotland turned away from Catholicism the city was at the centre of the Reformation which paved the way for modern Scotland to develop. Sickened by the corruption and greed of a church which was responsible for the administration of justice and which had turned Scotland into a satellite of Catholic France, Scots of all classes sought change.

It came with the revolutionary doctrines of Martin Luther. His works were banned by the

Colonel Arbuthnott, Secretary of the Black Watch Association and (above) the first Black Watch uniform

Scottish Parliament and the heresy of preaching of his views was punishable by death. But discontent with the established order grew and the ports of the Tay secretly imported Protestant tracts hidden among their cargoes from the Low Countries. In 1544 Cardinal Beaton sought to quell the mutinous citizens of Perth by hanging five men and drowning one woman for heresy.

Fifteen years later Perth had its revenge when John Knox, infuriated at the persecution of Protestants, preached his famous sermon in St John's Kirk, thus marking the beginning of the end of Catholic Scotland. Whipped up by Knox's inflammatory denunciation of idolatry, the people of Perth went on the rampage, destroying monasteries, friaries and religious sites. The Reformation had begun and Perth's historic role in it may help to explain why, even to this day and unusually for this part of Scotland, the Orange Order maintains a significant following in the city.

During the Jacobite risings of 1715 and 1745, Perth supported the Stuart bid for the restoration of the Scottish throne. The fact that Bonnie Prince Charlie was a Catholic was outweighed by resentment of the political clout of the Campbell clan which was favoured by the Westminster government following the Union of 1707. During both rebellions the city first cheered advancing rebel armies and then gloomily witnessed their flight north, pursued by Hanoverian armies – and, on the first occasion, escaping across the iced-over waters of the Tay.

The Government's answer to the rebelliousness of the Highland clans was brutal repression. After the rebellion of 1715, General Wade constructed a network of roads and bridges linking Perth, Inverness and Fort William to allow the speedy advance of troops. Later, in a bid to stem growing discontent, loyal clansmen were recruited into a vigilante, armed police force. These irregulars, active in suppressing both Jacobites and endemic bandits, went on to become the Black Watch – one of the most famous and feared regiments in the British Army. First mustered in 1740 on the banks of the Tay at Aberfeldy, the Black Watch is the regiment of the Tay. Many of the first Gaelic-speaking recruits, however, believed that they had enlisted to stay in Scotland and showed little enthusiasm for fighting abroad for the British Empire. When they were marched south for the first time in 1743 a mutiny broke out in London and many of the Highlanders fled north. Some 107 men, 79 of whom spoke no English, were tried for mutiny; three were shot in the Tower of London in front of their comrades.

The regimental headquarters at Perth's Balhousie Castle includes a museum which is open to the public. Black Watch Association secretary Colonel David Arbuthnott stresses the links between the Tay and its fighting men: 'The Black Watch is a regiment that has fierce loyalties associated with it. Our battle honours stretch from the 1750s to the Korean War in the 1950s. The regiment was formed in Aberfeldy prior to the '45 and it is said that if the Black Watch had not been withdrawn from the area to fight in France, the '45 uprising would not have occurred.

'The regiment has taken in people from around Perthshire, Angus and Fife since 1881, so I suppose it is a Tay Valley regiment rather than a Highland one. I don't think that there is a single town or a village around the Tay which has a memorial to the two World Wars that doesn't feature a large number of Black Watch members. The regiment has a long association with the area. In the 1920s, just after the First World War, I would imagine that virtually every family in the Tay area had some connection with the regiment.'

The current strength of the Black Watch is around 1,000 regular soldiers, with a further

400 Territorial Army members of the regiment reporting to a number of TA bases around the Tay. Such is the fighting record of the regiment – not to mention its popularity – that no Government minister has ever dared propose its disbandment as a part of defence cuts. The regimental museum draws around 10,000 visitors each year, many of them ex-servicemen and their families. Colonel Arbuthnott outlines its appeal: 'The museum epitomises the character of the regiment and the character of the people in it. Members of the Black Watch were, and are, renowned for their steadiness, firmness, courage and endurance in difficult times. The museum has existed since 1925 and has been at Balhousie since 1962. The exhibits of pictures, weapons, uniforms and documents celebrate the long tradition of the regiment and I would estimate that the collection is priceless. We also have a special library to which visitors may have access by appointment. Every soldier who joins the Black Watch comes to Balhousie for a day and we hope that they are inspired by the acts of their predecessors.'

The Black Watch is a living reminder of Tayside's turbulent past, a history at odds with the comfortable, secure county town of today. Perth's elegant Georgian crescents, parks and fine historical buildings invite comparison with Scotland's modern capital, inspiring many residents to proudly refer to their home city as a 'mini-Edinburgh'. The survival and refurbishment of so many of Perth's fine old buildings in the face of the combined onslaught of modern architecture and property developers is largely thanks to a rear-guard action fought by a force just as redoubtable as the Black Watch. To echo the regimental motto, nobody provokes the Perth Civic Trust with impunity. For 25 years the Civic Trust has battled to save and conserve Perth's architectural heritage. Its battle honours include the riverside Commercial Street, the Old Academy building in Rose Terrace and the Round House, which now houses the Fergusson art collection.

Elwena Fraser, a founder member of the Trust and a past chairperson, can take satisfaction from the results of a classic campaigning pressure group. She recalls: 'In July 1968 I received a call from the late Dr Margaret Stewart, an eminent Scottish archaeologist and personal friend. She said that the council was planning to demolish the old Ferry House, a Georgian building down by the river in Commercial Street, which was then a run-down area. About six or seven of us met in Margaret's home. We were all fairly angry. The council had earlier demolished the Earl of Kinnoull's old house in the Watergate and now they proposed to knock down the old Ferry House. Unfortunately, there was an attitude among council officials that if a building was over 80 years old, it was a danger to the public and should be demolished. We felt that we had to act to save what was left of Perth.'

What was to become the Civic Trust lost its battle to save the Ferry House, but subsequently had a big say in the redevelopment of Commercial Street. The Trust ensured that photographs of condemned buildings were recorded for posterity, and organised Sunday walks around Perth to raise local awareness of a unique heritage. 'We also felt it was important to involve young people and bring in the schools,' says Elwena. 'Children were encouraged to paint Perth's historic vennels and write little books on local history. We took classes in schools and even became part of a Sixth-Year Studies course at Perth Academy.'

The Trust was able to win support for the establishment of conservation areas within Perth and influenced plans for the city centre to ensure that redevelopment was sympathetic to the city's existing architecture. Gradually, the Trust won admiration from former foes for its persistence and persuasive skills. The campaign to save the Round House marked a turning point. As Elwena stresses, 'The Round House, which is now a marvellous home for the

Elwena Fraser outside the Round House, now home to the
Fergusson Collection

Fergusson collection, would have been a pile of rubble if we had not stepped in. It is also a memorial to the Perth Civic Trust and something of which we can be proud. When it was handed to the town by the Water Board nobody knew what to do with it. One councillor suggested that it should be knocked down and I remember going home in tears. We were determined not only to save the building but to find a use for it. We commissioned an architect to redesign it and wrote to everyone we could think of. Eventually, the Tourist Board found it useful as a temporary home.'

Perth's first female Provost counts herself among the admirers of the Civic Trust. Appointed in 1992, Mrs Jean McCormack, Perth's new civic head, is a long-standing councillor from the Carse of Gowrie. Although a Conservative, she sees her role of Provost as non-political but has benefited from Perth's apparent good fortune, almost alone in Scotland, in having profited from the Thatcher years.

Jean is enthusiastic about the town's renaissance: 'Perth has undergone a major transformation in the last few years and, through initiatives such as the Perth Partnership, which draws together the private and public sectors, and Perth in Bloom, we have made great efforts to ensure that the city looks its best. Apart from the pedestrianisation of the High Street and the changes in the commercial part of the city, we have greatly improved Perth's parks. On the banks of the river we have opened up an old walkway leading to the Rodney Pavilion and park. The next upgrading we are considering is widening the pavements of Tay Street and creating a boulevard-style atmosphere. In fact, Perth achieves a Parisian feel already, especially in May when artists display their works on the riverside railings.'

Appropriately for the Provost of a city which owes its very existence to the Tay, Jean has a special attachment to the river which allowed the city to develop as a trading centre and crossing place. 'The Tay is one of Perth's most important tourism attractions,' she says. 'We are considering reintroducing Black Swans on to the river. The original Black Swans were gifted by our twin town of Perth, Australia, but they disappeared. The council chambers have a balcony looking out over the river and people find it very relaxing to walk there after a tense debate. The river has a calming influence. I come from Dundee originally and have always been very close to the river.'

Douce though Perth may be, its citizens have nonetheless displayed a remarkable entrepreneurial ability. The giant General Accident insurance company has its world headquarters in its home town and now employs a staff of 17,000 servicing millions of policies in 45 countries worldwide. More recently, transport deregulation produced a niche which allowed Ann Gloag to build her Stagecoach empire; she now runs 3,000 buses on four continents and employs 11,000 people. Perth's long-running involvement in whisky (the Perth Guild admitted Ellice MacKerane, its first 'aquavitae maker', in 1561) continues and the city is the headquarters of United Distillers and Matthew Gloag, renowned for its Famous Grouse blend.

For all that, Perth is an unusually pleasing blend of the old and the new. Retaining a countrified couthiness, it serves the fertile hinterlands of Kinross, Strathearn and the Tay Valley. The solicitors' practices and firms of land agents which developed to serve prosperous farmers and great estates still give Perth the feel of an authentic county town and the city's twice-yearly bull sales have become legendary, attracting huge prices for prime Aberdeen Angus breeding stock. Its status as an agricultural market town was enhanced by Perth Harbour, which allowed the bulk shipping of agricultural produce.

Perth people have been shrewd traders and merchants for centuries. For hundreds of years the Tay and its tributaries were the only effective highways into the Highlands, and when, in the thirteenth century, the East of Scotland from Aberdeen to Berwick was enjoying unprecedented power and wealth, Perth was centre stage. Thirty miles from the sea, Perth's tidal harbour was first promoted by Royal Charter in 1137 and allowed the import of flax and the export of hides and leather goods. Later, in the eighteenth century, the town became famous for its trade in gloves. During the same period, iced salmon was sent south by ship, with two vessels a week making the journey to London at the height of the salmon season. A record of 60 hours for the voyage was established in 1796. The harbour, originally near the centre of Perth, once had a shipbuilding industry and timber was floated down the river to supply the yard. Shipbuilding has long ceased, though, and gradually the port moved downstream to its current location near Friarton.

Since 1982 Perth Harbour has been in the charge of Captain Norman Lawrance, who took up the challenge after 34 years at sea. In the decade since he has witnessed big changes at the

Captain Norman Lawrance, Perth Harbour Master

The launch of the schooner Jessie Meck *at Perth, 1872*

port: 'In 1982 the harbour dealt with between 75 and 100 ships each year. The cargoes were mostly farm-related, and consisted of fertilizers, animal fodder, barley and the like. The harbour has diversified now and in 1990 we dealt with 320 vessels. They are larger and are trading door-to-door in the European Community. Prior to 1982 we could only handle ships of around 100 tonnes but now we can accommodate vessels of 2,000 tonnes. The harbour can take much larger vessels than its appearance suggests. During the Miners' Strike of 1984 we handled ships with cargoes of between 14,000 and 16,000 tonnes. Agricultural cargoes are still very much our bread and butter but we also export steel plate and import coal, fuels, steel, chemicals, paper and timber products.'

Investment by the owners, Tayside Regional Council, has expanded the port by adding 33 metres of berth to the quays which are built on reclaimed land. New warehouses, offices and workshops add to the bustling atmosphere of a facility few visitors to the Gateway to the Highlands would ever imagine existed. But, as Captain Lawrance explains, the port still has to overcome natural difficulties: 'The harbour is well sheltered but the tide is our main enemy. In the winter, when the neap or low tides occur, the level of water drops so much that not a great deal of work can be done. The tidal period is very short and the river is busy with comings and goings. Movements have to be carefully co-ordinated with as many as nine vessels taking advantage of the tide. Unlike coastal ports we are also at the mercy of the amount of water coming down the river. Spates can alter sandbanks and a five-knot flow during these spates can make harbour work extremely difficult.'

Perth's location may be advantageously central but it has also been rather 'out of sight, out of mind' as far as the trades union movement is concerned. Perth harbour's 'non-scheme' status meant it was free of National Dock Labour Board regulations, a factor which contributed to its growth. Similar factors allowed Perth to steal a march in another transport industry, namely coach services. Trades unions were alert to the threat posed to jobs and services by bus deregulation but never expected that Britain's major new private player would materialise in Perth.

Ann Gloag, backed by her bus-driver father's redundancy money, spotted her chance and went on to build her company into a multimillion-pound business. Stagecoach began with just one second-hand bus in 1980 and has grown to operate a massive fleet of coaches across Britain with several hundreds abroad. The figures of the Stagecoach success story speak for themselves: assets are valued at £25 million, turnover is £160 million annually and operating profit is £13 million. Unsurprisingly, Ann was voted Britain's Businesswoman of the Year in 1991 and was named European Woman of Achievement the following year. In 1993 Stagecoach was floated on the Stock Exchange attracting 30,000 investors who parted with over £130 million for a piece of the action.

Stagecoach now has operations in Malawi, Kenya, China, Vietnam, Canada and Sri Lanka. In 1992 it became the first company in Britain to operate a privatised rail service by winning a franchise to offer seats on the Aberdeen to London service.

As group managing director, Ann leads a hectic lifestyle which takes her round the world but she is always pleased to talk about her home town. 'I have lived in Perth all my life,' she declares proudly. 'Before we started Stagecoach I worked in Bridge of Earn hospital as a theatre sister. I would never live anywhere other than Perth but I admit I am biased. With its river setting the city is very picturesque and is well provided for with its theatre and leisure facilities. Our group headquarters is based in Perth and the location has no disadvantage for an international operation at all. It is extremely convenient for airports and is basically a lovely place to live. I suppose I really should walk by the Tay and take advantage of the area's beautiful scenery but when I've been travelling all week my favourite thing is to sit back and enjoy the company of my family at home. I look forward to the day then I will actually be able to enjoy this area to the full.'

The striking success of Stagecoach does not obscure the fact that much of Perth's thriving business community owes its vitality to traditional activities and industries. The Perth bull sales, for example, built their worldwide fame on the quality of Scottish pure-bred cattle and on that of the Aberdeen Angus in particular. Perth has exported Aberdeen Angus livestock to destinations as far-flung as China and Argentina, worthy bovine ambassadors of Scottish farming skill. The commercial know-how required for the hundred year build-up of the sales has come from three generations of one family, the Frasers. Auctioneering began in Perth in the 1850s and by 1875, when John Maclaren Fraser was appointed managing director of the

Sheep shearing, Perth Mart, May 1948

principal firm of auctioneers, the city was a well-established sales centre for horses, sheep and cattle. Mr Fraser continued in the business until 1938, shortly before his death at the age of 95. The business he established, now United Auctions, is in the hands of Roley Fraser. A third-generation auctioneer, he has recently overseen the move to spanking new premises on the outskirts of town.

At his new base in the Perth Agricultural Centre at East Huntingtower, Roley relates the scale of the changes which will keep Perth to the fore of the livestock industry in the next century: 'The total cost of the new development was £6.5 million, including the purchase of the 33-acre site. The new premises have been constructed with all the latest modern facilities and ample parking space for up to 1,400 vehicles. We moved here in 1990 because the old site near the centre of town was getting too congested with livestock now moving by road rather than rail. The new centre represents a major investment and it really was necessary. The whole emphasis is now on roads and the advent of the Perth bypass made this an ideal site.

'Perthshire is good stock country and the farmers have done a lot to improve the quality of the land and the livestock. There is some quite exceptional land up the length of the Tay.' Nevertheless, United Auctions deal in animals from across Scotland and, in increasing numbers, even from England. 'There has been a change in the types of livestock we sell. For example, we now sell eight different breeds of cattle. Perth is recognised by people from all over the world as a place to come and buy bulls, many of which are brought up from England. At the last February sale we sold 700 bulls with around 75 per cent of the beasts and 40 per cent of the buyers from south of the border. The sales are a very important part of the local community here and have a significant input into the local economy. Around 2,000 people attend the sales each February and October, so there is a fair knock-on for shops and hotels.

'We are hoping that the buildings here will eventually become a complete agricultural centre. We already have some shops and would like to broaden this with potato merchants, NFU offices and the like. Agriculture as a whole is depressed around the Tay at the moment but that is to do with general farming economics since the Second World War. Farmers were firstly encouraged to produce more and more and are now told that they are too efficient and are producing too much. Because of Perth's locality and the quality of the surrounding land, however, it will always be an agricultural centre. I still act as auctioneer at many of the sales, which I enjoy tremendously. I am working now with the third generation of farming families since I started. We have our own farm of 300 acres at Parkfield near Scone. It is run by my wife and we have been there for around 35 years. Although I can't stand fishing or sailing, the river is very beautiful and Perth offers a very good quality of life. The city is like a mini-Edinburgh and because it hasn't made any grandiose schemes for its waterfront, it lives and breathes well with the river.'

Local businessman Ian Thomson, an incomer to Perth from Glasgow, cheerfully supports Roley's estimation of the quality of life in Perth and of the rare abundance of its countryside. As a director of Taygame, he is involved in the export of produce from what he calls 'Scotland's finest natural larder' to destinations around the world. 'Customer feedback from our clients in Belgium, Holland, Germany, France and Italy is very positive,' he says. 'They are delighted with the quality of the product and we are able to get a premium price. People are prepared to pay a bit more for the pick of Tayside's game.'

Ian is emphatic that the success of his firm is due to the excellence of the local game. 'The

Ian Thomson of Taygame

quality of the land around the Tay makes for impressive game,' he stresses. 'Local estates are also very well managed and looked after by experienced gamekeepers. Rabbits are superb and pheasants are big, weighing in at 3 or 4 kilos.'

A keen shooter himself, Ian is evangelical: 'It is estimated that there are around 30 species of game available on the land of the Tay. The game sport is so good that local agencies bring in thousands of Italians to the area every year. They get very excited at what they see. They cannot imagine that there is so much high-quality game here and their arrival, mainly in the winter, is a welcome boost to local businesses. The good news is that growing numbers of local people are beginning to appreciate that wild game is one of the few purely natural food sources left. It is a natural wholesome food.'

Ian would never dream of moving from an area where he can combine his business and his hobbies. Perth's citizens, even its adopted ones, take a justified pride in their city. Throughout the 1980s and 1990s, it has developed its leisure, shopping, hotel and restaurant facilities, winning national recognition in offering one of Britain's finest lifestyles. The city's refurbished repertory theatre is well supported, and pleasant walks have been created by the riverbank and at Bell's Cherrybank Gardens.

Perth's modern leisure centre and swimming pool is one of the region's most visited amenities and the establishment of Dewar's Rinks has consolidated the Fair City's reputation as a centre for curling. The upsurge in civic pride has been mirrored by the fortunes of St Johnstone, Perth's football team which was founded in 1884 and is the proud possessor of Scottish football's newest stadium.

Local businessman Geoff Brown made his fortune building the new homes which house

Perth's growing population. But, since 1986, he has devoted much of his energy to building St Johnstone, the team he has supported since he was a boy. Devoid of the egocentric tycoonery and buffoonery which characterises so many self-styled soccer 'saviours', Geoff is a popular and modest chairman who has steadily built up his side and delights in talking about the city he loves: 'I was born in the Barnhill part of Perth and am a real native of this area. I moved to Glencarse in the Carse of Gowrie in 1971. I live in a house close to my builder's yard between the river and the railway line, a very pleasant location from which to work. I used to fish on the river as a boy but between my business and St Johnstone, I don't have enough time these days.

'I took charge at St Johnstone in 1986 and there have been a lot of changes since then. I have supported the team since I was a lad and it was a really great opportunity for me. My investment in the club has been more in time than in money, because we were able to sell the previous site at Muirton Park. But it has been hard work. I would say that running a football club is in many ways the same as running a business: both require leadership and the ability to work as a team. If you treat people the way you expect to be treated and work well together, there is no end to the success you can achieve.'

He takes particular pride in the construction of St Johnstone's McDiarmid Park stadium: 'I believe that in McDiarmid Park we have one of the most advanced stadia in the country. The new stadium has had a positive knock-on effect on the quality of the football and is an important addition to the community which can be used by local people. It annoys me when people go on about Ibrox. When Rangers chairman David Murray said to me that we were two of the most forward-thinking clubs in the country, I replied that the honour belonged to St Johnstone alone because our stadium is completely new, while his is second-hand!

Chuck Hay, Perth Ice Rink

'McDiarmid Park is the only stadium in Britain to fully comply with the Taylor report; we moved here in July 1989 just three months after the Hillsborough tragedy which led to the Taylor recommendations. At the end of the last season all we had to do was reseed the pitch and test 25 per cent of the crush barriers and that was it. Every other ground in the country had to do much more. I would say that Perth has undergone a real transformation in the last few years and it is now definitely a city of the 1990s. I am pleased that St Johnstone has been part of the transformation.'

In Perth's sporting world that transformation has not been confined to football. Nearby St Andrews may be the birthplace of golf, but Perth can lay claim to a game just as royal and every bit as ancient. Curling, one of the world's oldest winter sports, began in the area five hundred years ago with later written records of the game being played at Muthil and Kinross dating from around 1600. The 'roaring game', so named because of the noise of the granite stones sliding across frozen loch surfaces, was especially popular in Victorian times when virtually every castle and big house in the Carse of Gowrie and Tay Valley had a curling pond. Local clubs tended to be located at the Laird's house, allowing a rare opportunity for villagers and landlords to mix. Queen Victoria was so impressed by this aspect of the game when she visited Scone Palace that she conferred the royal seal of approval on the Grand Caledonian Curling Club.

The demise of Scotland's sharp, severe winters played a role in diminishing the popularity of the sport after the Second World War. Even with the advent of hydro-electric dams on the Tay's tributaries, which have slowed the flow of the river, it would be unthinkable today that curling tournaments, tea-parties and ox roasts could be held on the frozen waters of the Tay between Perth's bridges as they were in the last century.

Over the last two decades, however, the sport – sometimes referred to as 'bowls on ice' – has enjoyed a remarkable revival. Curling is now a highly competitive game which attracts growing numbers of women and young people and is mainly played on indoor rinks where the ice is more consistent. Scotland now has around 50,000 curlers, some 5,000 of whom live in the Perth area and enjoy the unique facilities of Dewar's Rinks. The rinks, like Bell's Cherrybank Gardens, are a product of the generosity of United Distillers, who donated the site for a development which cost £5.2 million.

The chairman of Dewar's Rinks is Chuck Hay, whose son David led his Perth team to victory in the 1991 world championships in Winnipeg. Perthshire-born and bred, Chuck runs the family farm at Easter Rhynd. Sandwiched between the Tay and the Earn and established a century ago by his grandfather, the farm includes 300 acres of rich alluvial soil reclaimed from the Tay. Chuck enjoys sailing up the river to tend the sluice gates on his land and loves walking along its banks in the spring – but his greatest passion is curling.

He delights in revealing some of the complexities of a game he discovered by accident while immobilised by a rugby injury: 'Until 1950 players used their own stones but now ice-rinks have their own set of 64, all cut from the same column of granite to eliminate advantage. The stones were traditionally made from Ailsa Craig granite, but for a long time manufacturers were using Welsh granite which is more porous and wears more easily. Happily, Ailsa Craig granite is available again. They make the Rolls-Royce of curling stones. Good stones run more easily and the running surface lasts longer. Curling is a tough sport and can be a tremendous physical and mental strain. The Perth rink is a superb modern facility. The difference between playing in a modern rink and outdoors is vast. Outdoor curling is like playing golf in a cobbled street.'

Chuck 'skipped' the first Scottish team ever to win the World Championship in 1967 and spent 14 years as chief umpire at the World Championships before being made President of the Royal Caledonian Curling Club. His enthusiasm for the game remains undiminished and he is pleased by its new-found popularity: 'Curling has really changed from the days when it was viewed as an old man's sport. If you are over 35 you have no chance in a competitive sense! There are lots of youngsters involved now. We have 16 schools competing on a regular league basis and a junior championship sponsored by the Bank of Scotland. I am extremely proud that the world champions are from Perth. They have been an inspiration to the curling community in the city and have played a role in increasing the popularity of the sport.'

The new Dewar's rinks, Perth's popular leisure pool and modern indoor sports facilities are fast earning the city a reputation as a leisure and sports venue. But some attractions have been around a lot longer. Like most Scottish cities, Perth is well served by its golf courses and the King James VI Club is in a category all of its own. As Club captain Tony Coles explains, 'This is the only golf course in the world which is built on a natural island within a city boundary. There is only one other like it – in Perth, Australia, funnily enough – but it is on a *man-made* island within the city boundaries. Ours is unusual and a bit of a novelty. There is a causeway which allows us to get the occasional car across during low tide but the main access is by the footbridge.'

The club moved in 1897 from a municipal course on the North Inch, where King James VI once played 'gowf' with his nobles, to Moncrieffe Island. The club shares the island – which is about one and a half miles long and less than half a mile wide – with a green-fingered community of allotment-holders who occupy a quarter of the island. Demand for membership is high. The club membership of 675 is fully subscribed and the waiting-list is closed.

Tony elaborates on the club's attractions: 'This is a nice, flat easy course and it is not expensive. There is huge demand for golf courses in this area. Generally speaking, there is no real problem being situated on an island. We have good drainage and a nice clubhouse with the full range of facilities open all day, seven days a week. Every 50 years or so we do get flooded, and in 1990 the clubhouse was like an island, with the steward stranded by the rising waters. We are very busy with members and visitors and it is a lovely place to be.'

The city also has its fair share of attractions for the less athletically inclined. Gardening enthusiasts and nature-lovers can not only stroll along imaginatively landscaped parkland walks but can enjoy two of Scotland's finest gardens at Branklyn and Cherrybank. The National Trust's Branklyn Garden was once famed as the best small town garden of under two acres in Britain. Under the direction of administrator Bob Mitchell it is currently being restored to its former glory – not that its present condition fails to please the 19,000 visitors who soak up its tranquillity and beauty each year.

A professional horticulturalist and former curator of the University of St Andrews Botanic Garden, Bob feels doubly privileged in both working at Branklyn and living in the grounds of a wonderful garden. This small garden – designed and developed by Perth couple John and Dorothy Renton over a 40-year period – contains an astonishing 3,000 species. It also has 150 varieties of rhododendron which herald the arrival of spring with a riot of colour.

Vasart employees, Shore Road works, Perth c.*1950*

Monart collector, James Jackson

'I have known this place for almost 40 years, first coming here as a student back in 1955 when I met the Rentons who bequeathed the garden to the National Trust for Scotland,' says Bob. 'They were always very appreciative of the visitors who came to enjoy the garden. For me, the most important aspects of the garden are its design by John Renton, its exciting range of plants, especially from the Sino-Himalayan area and the sheer number of visitors we receive – a lot for a wee garden.'

Branklyn, one of Perth's longest-established gardens, is complemented by a newcomer across the river, Bell's Cherrybank Garden, at the site of United Distillers offices. These imaginatively designed 18 acres were first opened to the public in 1988 and, with no charge for admission, have proved immensely popular with local people and visitors alike. In 1992, some 46,000 visitors took in the sights at Cherrybank during its season from May to October.

The garden includes the world's largest collection of heathers, 700 in all, and the team of gardeners headed by Norrie Robertson is determined to increase this to 1,000. The garden, which needs between one and two hours to be seen fully, is influenced by a water theme and has six large ponds containing goldfish and trout, fountains and an acoustic pool. A miniature Crystal Palace contains an aviary for a mixed flock of budgerigars and cockatiels, and in one of the trellis gardens there is a set of tubular bells.

Public art in the shape of sculptures by Ian Hamilton Findlay, Laurence Broderick, Sadie McLellan and Iain Mackintosh has pride of place at Cherrybank. Pedestrianisation of Perth's main shopping street has included a striking sculpture by David Annand, inspired by the work of William Soutar, the Perth poet who spent much of his life paralysed, ill in bed.

Soutar aside, Perth can lay few claims to any kind of literary heritage. In the visual arts, however, generations of Perth silversmiths earned a reputation for skilled craftsmanship and, earlier this century, the city made one of Scotland's most notable contributions to the Art Deco movement in the form of ornamental Monart glass. Now hugely collectable, Monart glass and, more often, its inferior successor Vasart, can still be found in Perth's numerous antique shops. Monart glass has won a following around the world with collectors' clubs in Perth, Australia and in the United States. Both the Queen and the Queen Mother are avid collectors and Perth's gift to the Queen on her wedding was a Monart decanter and glasses. It is also popular in France and Italy, where some items can fetch thousands of pounds.

Antique-dealer James Jackson specialises in the glass and has become something of an authority. He takes up the Monart story: 'Salvador Ysart, the creator of Monart, arrived in Perth in the 1920s. He and his family had worked their way through glassworks across Europe from their home in Barcelona. He took up a job at the Moncrieff glassworks which are still located at St Catherine's Road in Perth. Salvador brought a number of Spanish glassmaking skills with him, but he didn't start commercially making the coloured glass immediately. The owner's wife, Marion Moncrieffe spotted him making some pieces for his friends and liked them so much that she got him to make it, originally, for her friends. Monart takes its name from the first part of Moncrieffe and the last part of Ysart.'

James scours the country seeking out examples of the prized glass which was produced from 1924 in over 300 shapes and 500 colour patterns. Initially only vases and bowls were produced but demand persuaded the glassworks to manufacture lemonade jugs, perfume bottles, ink bottles and lamps. In the last few years prices for Monart have shot up. As James explains, 'The glass is highly coloured. In the early days the colours were more subtle but later they became wilder and gold foil was flecked through the glass during various stages of its production. You can really see the influence of Spanish and French glass in it. The colours are exciting with good strong shapes but the pieces are very practical.

'An average bowl or vase starts at £60 and good paperweights are worth a few hundred pounds. A Monart mushroom lamp was sold for £3,000 recently. There is a big difference between prices for a run-of-the-mill piece and the special pieces that were made for exhibitions.'

Eventually, Salvador, a fiery character, left Moncrieff with two of his sons to open his own works by the Tay. Another son, Paul, stayed at Moncrieff to make paperweights which are now famous worldwide as collector's items costing up to £800. The new Ysart factory adapted to shortages of European materials during the war and, using river water and sand, developed Vasart as the successor to Monart.

'I've heard,' recounts James, 'that when the family was based by the Tay, they used the river to get rid of a lot of paperweights they were not happy with. Seemingly, they used to skim them across the water's surface. I would imagine that there is a few thousand pounds' worth lying in the sandbanks of the river.

'It is a pity that the glassware is still very underrated in Perth,' says James, regretfully. 'People look at it now and remember that their granny had a piece of it. There are some good local collectors but it is sad that the pieces are leaving the area where they originated.'

Perth's place in the Scottish art world has been assured, however, by the opening of the Fergusson Gallery. This unique collection and archive of a leading 'Scottish colourist' runs to an amazing 6,000 items and has an estimated value of £30 million. Awareness of the importance of John Duncan Fergusson in the development of Scottish art has grown over the last two decades, and the establishment of the gallery in Perth is a considerable coup for the city. Fergusson was born in Edinburgh but his parents came from Pitlochry and the artist always loved the Perthshire countryside. After his death in 1961 a trust was established to administer the substantial collection of oil paintings, watercolours, drawings, sketch books and sculptures inherited by his widow. The J. D. Fergusson Art Foundation worked for almost 30 years to make Fergusson's work more widely known. In 1990 it sought a permanent home for the collection and a proposal by Perth and Kinross District Council to locate it in the old 'A'-listed Perth Water Works was accepted.

Kirsten Simister, keeper of the collection in the Round House, explains the appeal of Fergusson's work: 'It is very joyful, celebratory, colourful and decorative. Fergusson was a very important influence in Scottish art. He spent a lot of time in Paris during the early part of this century and came in contact with the Parisian avant-garde. He was drawn towards the Fauvist school of painting which included Matisse and Derain.

'The gallery is the largest and single most important collection of Fergusson's work in existence. But he was extremely prolific and a lot of his works are elsewhere, and many are in private hands. Ultimately, we would like to attract bequests and build up our holding. The gallery will also act as a centre for research into Fergusson, his life and work. We have a large archive with several hundred photographs and several thousand press-clippings and letters.'

The unusual choice of the Round House for a gallery has not diminished public interest: 'A lot of people are very interested in the building itself,' says Kirsten. 'It was built in 1832 but has been adapted beautifully to a gallery function. Circular galleries are interesting and this one has a nice, almost domestic scale and intimate feel – which is good since a lot of Fergusson's

The artist in his studio: J. D. Fergusson, c.1905

work was very small. We like to have a friendly, informal atmosphere where people won't feel inhibited and can enjoy the collection.'

Not all of Perth's institutions are so friendly or so informal. Just along the river from the Fergusson Gallery, the grim buttresses of Perth Prison constitute an historic building that rarely finds its way into tourist brochures and guides. But Perth Prison is one of the city's most important employers and best-known landmarks. The current site of the prison was formerly home to a miserable prisoner-of-war camp for over 7,000 French prisoners between 1810 and 1815. The prisoners drained the marshy ground next to the river, where they lived and died in appalling conditions. Hundreds, if not thousands, perished at the Perth camp.

The first records of a prison proper at Perth go back to 1836, and although the prison as we know it today was built in 1842, the myth of its construction by Napoleonic prisoners persists. Up until this time there was little need for a Central Prison of Scotland, as the Perth jail was known. Long-term 'criminals' were simply either hanged or transported, and a large number of small local prisons catered for petty offenders. Perth prison was the first of its type and is Scotland's oldest penal establishment.

Around 450 prisoners are held at Perth in Victorian prison buildings. They share their stark surroundings with 400 prison officers and staff. For generations of Taysiders, Perth has been synonymous with its prison – and for Dundee's criminal fraternity the expression 'going up the river' has carried a degree of dread. 'The prison is an important aspect of Perth,' says

Governor Ron Kite. 'I would imagine that there are very few local people who don't have some connection with the prison. We are one of the city's top ten employers and the yearly budget is almost £12 million.

'The depot or billet for the French prisoners of war which existed here between 1810 and 1815 was a basic shed. Many of them had to march from Tayport to Perth after being dropped off by ship, and others stopped off at a church in Inchture where they carved their mark. A fair number of them died while they were here and when new walls were constructed for the prison in the 1970s, bodies of the Napoleonic PoWs were discovered and a plaque was erected to their memory.

Long-serving Officer Instructor David Haggart has researched the history of the prison he has worked in for almost two decades: 'The prison was built on this site because the docks are very near and it was easier to transport the stone that way. When foundations were dug for new construction, large vaults were found. It was rumoured that these might have been tunnels which led directly to the river, but it is more likely that they were routes into the prison after the prisoners were dropped off by boat. This area is still referred to as the "Military Walk".

'There used to be a tower at the centre of the prison, but only the base is left. Originally, there was a market square inside the prison where the inmates used to sell their produce to the locals. The foundations for the original building were built on rafts of straw, which must have been laid as some protection against the Tay flooding. These rafts were constructed from local reeds and, even now, the fields around the prison will flood during extremely high tides.'

The fickleness of the Tay affects the town as much as the prison. In the thirteenth century the ancient city was virtually destroyed by flooding. Carved into the red sandstone of Smeaton's Bridge at Perth are the flood levels in modern times, the highest recorded in February 1814 at more than 21 feet above the river-bank. Most floods occur between December and January. The most recent, in January 1993, was just 18 inches short of the 1814 record on Smeaton's bridge. In Perth, the North and South Inches, the harbour quays, Moncrieffe island, city centre streets and, most heartbreakingly, hundreds of homes on the North Muirton estate were inundated. The total bill for damage may reach an astonishing £50 million. The agricultural bill for washed away farms is assessed at £12 million, the housing damage at £15 million and repairs to roads, water services, rail links and bridges is put at £10 million and rising.

The flood waters of the Tay receded within days but amid the chaos and debris left behind by the unleashed power of the river, the victims had only one question: will it happen again? Provost Jean McCormack believes: 'We cannot give any guarantees'. Ron Allcock, director of the Perth-based Tay River Purification Board, is more direct. He says bluntly, 'Sooner or later it will happen again. These are not freak events.'

Politicans are under pressure to tame the Tay but the political backwash of the floods of 1993 poses the inevitable – and so far unanswered – question as to who will pick up the tab for a flood-prevention programme which could cost more than the damage of the worst floods this century. Perth may have begun life as a crossing place over the Tay but in 1993 it became a bottleneck on the river's unstoppable rush to the sea, with an astonishing 40,000 million gallons of water a day pouring through the town at the height of the flood. Upstream, hydro-electric dams held back a further 130,000 million gallons and hundreds of acres of farmland were flooded, relieving the pressure on the Fair City. The flow of water recorded on the Tay at Ballathie on 16 January 1993 was almost 2,000 cubic metres a second, the highest recorded figure for any river in Britain.

Farmers, who were told that the earlier floods of 1990 were a 'once-in-a-century' occurrence, ruefully contemplated fields submerged for the second time in three years, and householders on the stricken North Muirton estate endured months of living in temporary accommodation as their homes were dried out and rebuilt. The first step in preventing it all from happening again, Ron Allcock believes, is impressing upon politicians the unique nature of the Tay. 'They must appreciate the sheer scale of a river system which drains 8,000 square kilometres of the south-eastern Highlands and embraces 70 lochs and 6,500 kilometres of river,' he stresses.

'At the time of the 1990 floods, we went to meetings and heard people talking about once in a hundred years. We warned that it could happen again and that it could be worse. We have noticed a climatic change in the board's area. There is nothing to stop the sequence of rain-snow-rain happening again. It happened in 1990 and, to a lesser extent, in 1992. Over the past ten years the winters have become wetter and the base water level of the Tay has increased by 15 per cent during the winter. Luckily for Perth, we had a very low tide during the 1993 floods. The tide was only three metres high – had it been a high tide of around five metres the situation would have been much more serious.

'Investment for flood prevention must be made available. It is all about money, and big money at that. But Perth may be dealing with flood alerts on an annual basis and we have to take this seriously.'

His sentiments are echoed by Provost McCormack who accepts that the floods of 1993 were not a freak: 'In 1990 people gambled that the floods were a once-in-a-lifetime event and they didn't reinsure. It is true that the authorities also gambled and did not take the problem seriously enough. The Government has to appreciate the scale of what happened here. People are terrified if it snows in January and February and live in fear of the spring tides in March.'

The authorities have now dusted off a report commissioned in the wake of the 1990 floods and are facing up to the problem with renewed urgency. Reconstruction of flood banks and barriers to a higher level, dredging, the construction of new dams, and the flooding of tracts of floodplain are among the options to be considered. Each of these, however, presents a new problem. Damming would submerge upriver communities like Killin and Kenmore; dredging might destroy the salmon fishing; more flood embankments could channel the river into a fiercer torrent leading to flooding in the flatlands of the Carse of Gowrie; and the use of floodplains involves compensating farmers and, in any event, manifestly failed in 1993. As a first step, a further study of the entire river network, at a probable cost of £250,000 is to be commissioned and a computer model of the river system constructed.

There are no easy answers to the taming of the Tay and certainly no cheap ones, but the experience of 1990 prompted the Purification Board to introduce a flood warning system to measure the rate of the river's rise. With the aid of a grant from Tayside Regional Council, a string of computerised warning stations has been established upriver from Perth. As Dr John Anderson of the Board's hydrology section explains, 'Our flood warning system twins reading instruments with computers. Wells are set into the river with a float to measure water level. When the level is high, an alarm is triggered at our headquarters. We can then phone the computer at the station which records all the data digitally and find out flow, levels, time span and the like so that we can warn people if the river is at a dangerous stage.

'By collecting day-to-day information from these stations we are able to build up a picture of the mean daily discharges of the river. It provides us with a statistical building block on which all hydrological information is based. Our information is helpful to civil engineers building bridges, it is of use to fish farmers and helps work out likely pollution levels.'

Despite the drama of the floods, it is the latter which most exercises the Tay River Purification Board. Modern farming with its reliance on nitrogen-based fertilisers, pesticides and herbicides mean that even stretches of the river in natural-looking rural environments can harbour high levels of toxins. Industry in Perth and Dundee discharges effluent which has to be monitored for its metal and pollutant content. Finally, dozens of outfalls pump raw sewage into the river – a practice gradually coming to an end with the imposition of strict European Community guidelines.

'The Tay is a very clean river,' says Ron Allcock. 'The Scottish Office classifies the cleanliness of rivers from 1 to 4 and the Tay rates a 1 right up to Invergowrie. Estuaries are rated A to D and the Tay is a B, principally because there are 36 outfalls of crude sewage from the Dundee area into the estuary. Steady progress is being made to improve treatment plants. We do have powers to prosecute those who regularly pollute and this year we have reported five cases to the procurator fiscal. The Tay remains the cleanest estuary in Europe and we intend to keep it that way.'

Chapter V

A WINDOW ON WILDLIFE

Leaving Perth and heading north, travellers today, as in centuries past, have little choice but to take the valley gouged out of the Grampian mountains by the Tay. In Scotland's bloody history control of the Great North Road which hugs the river was the key to the Highlands. The Romans fought their way upstream and peppered its banks with defensive forts. They reached as far north as Fortingall above Loch Tay, where Pontius Pilate is reputed to have been born. Centuries later the Danes followed until, at what is now called Denmarkfield, near Luncarty, they were overwhelmed. It was during that campaign to defeat the Norse invasion that Scotland adopted the symbol of the thistle, after a bare-footed invader reputedly stood on one of the prickly sentinels while crossing a sand-bar in the river to attack the sleeping Scottish army at Stanley. His yell of pain robbed the Danes of the element of surprise and allowed a Scottish victory.

For hundreds of years, until the arrival of 'law and order' after the '45, Strath Tay was the main route south for the gangs of marauding Highland bandits or caterans who periodically pillaged the wealthy lowlands. When these brigands became overactive, the powerful Bishops of Dunkeld would order the corpses of captured caterans to be hung from chains by the roadside to deter the south-bound raiders. In the rebellions of 1715 and 1745 thousands of Highland clansmen poured down this great glen to do battle with Government troops, only to flee north again in defeat and seek the protection of the mountains.

Today, an army of tourists brave the hazards of the A9 each summer to head for the hills of Perthshire or on to the Cairngorms and the Highland capital of Inverness. When it comes to scenery, they are rarely disappointed. The lush greenery of the lowland plain gradually gives way to a rugged grandeur which closes in on road and river.

Upstream from Perth, the river narrows and the current strengthens but the Tay remains subject to tidal rise as far as Woody Island, close to the original site of the Abbey of Scone to which English vessels paid customs in the twelfth century. Steeped in antiquity, Scone is at the heart of Scotland's story. Here the ancient Scots Parliament met and all 42 of Scotland's kings were crowned. The chosen spot was the Moot or Boot Hill near Scone Palace. This sizeable hummock is said to have been created by earth brought in on the boots of lords swearing loyalty to the king.

In the ninth century the Stone of Destiny was brought to Scone and many of the Scottish

A day at the races, Scone

kings were crowned on it before the English King, Edward, 'The Hammer of the Scots', seized the stone and installed it in Westminster Abbey. Despite having occupied a central place in Scottish folklore, it remained undisturbed there for 700 years, until Christmas Eve 1950 when four young Scottish Nationalist students created a sensation by 'liberating' the symbol of Scottish nationhood.

The Abbey and Bishop's House were destroyed in the disturbances that followed John Knox's Perth sermon in 1559 but the 'Palace of Scone', where the Scots kings stayed during coronations, survived and today forms magnificent Scone Palace in its splendid parkland setting. While architecturally undistinguished, the ancestral home of the Earls of Mansfield is literally a treasure-house of old paintings, fine porcelain, ivories, antique furniture and *objets d'art*.

The present Earl of Mansfield is listed by the *Sunday Times* as among Britain's wealthiest men, with an estimated private fortune of £45 to £50 million. Since inheriting the title in 1971, he and his wife, Lady Pamela, have turned Scone Palace into one of Scotland's premier visitor attractions. The estate's 30,000 acres are host to Britain's most northerly race course where each year huge numbers of visitors come to enjoy a day at the races. At the course located by the banks of the Tay, the Perth Hunt meets four times a year.

Clerk of the Course, Sam Morshead, has been delighted to note an increase in support for the Perth Hunt: 'Racing has a long history in this area. The first recorded race was the "Silver Bell", run in 1613 on the North Inch in Perth. Racing continued on the North Inch over the next three centuries and in 1908 it moved to Scone, where the Perth Hunt has been ever since. The course remains essentially the same and includes the only water jump left in Scotland. Situated just in front of the stand, it makes for a grand spectacle.'

The three-day Festival Meeting in April, an idea conceived by Sam, has helped bring greater numbers of both entrants and spectators from as far afield as Surrey, Sussex and Somerset. He explains, 'We try to create a bit of a party atmosphere with lots of extra activities such as ceilidhs, quiz nights and that sort of thing. Corporate hospitality is booming at Perth and, despite the recession, crowds have been increasing quite dramatically. The value of the races held has also been enhanced by increased sponsorship. Scone is known for its beautiful parkland setting, particularly in spring and autumn. It abounds with pheasants, hares and all kinds of wildlife. There is even a tale told of a Jockey Club starter who found time between races to nip down to the Tay and catch a salmon. It is an extremely pleasant setting.'

Close by, the village of Scone has now been all but absorbed into Perth and its unsightly forest of bed and breakfast signs tends to obscure local charm. The Air Training School is modern Scone's biggest claim to fame. Over the years it has taught thousands of mainly overseas students to fly and continues to flourish.

Scone is also home to Martin Brooks, one of the Tay's diminishing band of part-time pearl-fishers. When not on active duty with Perth's fire brigade, Martin is regularly to be found up to his waist in his favourite river clutching the pearl-fisher's primitive equipment of cleft stick and glass bucket. He is following in a tradition which stretches back 2,000 years. The Romans prized Scottish pearls above all others and the Scottish kings adorned their crowns with them. In recent years, however, pollution and overfishing have devastated stocks of the freshwater mussels which yield this treasure of the Tay. Now there are grounds for hope. Martin, some of his fellow pearl-fishers, and concerned scientists have successfully campaigned for new legislation to protect what are Europe's most important surviving colonies of *Margaritisera margaritisera*, a freshwater mollusc which can live up to 140 years.

During the 20 years in which he has scoured the river-bed, Martin has witnessed a sharp decline in stocks: 'I have seen the fishing on the Tay deteriorate over the years,' he says. 'There is far too much over-fishing and many of the beds are being killed off. I still come across the occasional large pearl but they are becoming harder to find. To get the big ones now, I have to fish the deep waters and that involves using sub-aqua equipment in the summer months when the water is not too cold.'

While Martin blames pollution from farm slurry and chemical sprays for damage to existing beds and also for preventing the growth of new colonies, his real ire is reserved for those fishers who kill thousands of mussels in pursuit of the 5 per cent which hold a pearl. 'I am pleased that we were able to bring about the introduction of legislation which makes it illegal to kill and destroy mussels. I just hope it will be adequately enforced. Policing will be the big problem. You do not have to kill the mussels – pearls can be extracted without damaging the shellfish. Yet, hardly any of the amateurs bother to replace them alive. They are killing the young mussels indiscriminately. It is sickening and still not uncommon to come across great piles of shells on the river-bank. We have to put a stop to these people and we must act quickly to keep the mussel beds that are left.'

Martin's sentiments are echoed by John Lochty, manager of Cairncross, the long-established Perth jeweller and supplier of Scottish pearl jewellery to the royal family. His firm buys pearls from the fishers, and experienced part-timers can easily earn £100 a day for their labours. A fine string of Scottish pearls can cost anything from £8,000 to £16,000. Small brooches can cost as little as £150 and the market for pieces of all sizes, quality and price is an encouraging one. John stresses that it is the uniqueness of the Scottish freshwater pearl which accounts for its popularity: 'They are completely distinct from cultured pearls. They have a different lustre. Because they are natural they come in all shapes and sizes, and literally every one is different. We can incorporate that individuality into our jewellery. That has a lot to do with the appeal of the pearls. There is a strong interest in the United States and Europe because people are looking for something different. We also have the famous "Little Willie" on display here. It weighs 33 grains and is 11 millimetres across. It is not the largest pearl – Christie's recently sold two which were larger – but it is the most perfect. It is difficult to calculate its value but some reports have mentioned the figure of £60,000.'

This stretch of the Tay, between Perth and Dunkeld, is probably the best for that other fishing for which the Tay is famed – salmon angling. Here, ghillies guide wealthy anglers by giving them the benefit of their pithy humour, as well as their expert knowledge of the dark pools where the salmon lie and wait before commencing the next stage of their journey upstream to the spawning grounds. The marked decline in salmon numbers has sparked a passionate controversy in which there is no shortage of culprits to blame. The latter include the riparian owners who profited from river netting and failed to re-stock the river sufficiently; English and Faroese drift-netters who scoop up thousands of salmon at sea; Russian factory ships which net vast quantities of sand-eels, on which the salmon feed at sea; anglers themselves and even environmentalists who have 'saved the seals' which gorge on salmon.

It is not just salmon that are hooked on the Tay: anglers can become addicted to the electric thrill of a bite and the beauty of their surroundings. One man's discovery of Tay salmon fishing 30 years ago has persuaded him to build a house by the river. Veteran journalist Arnott McWhinnie is chief crime reporter for the *Daily Record* and spends his working life probing the murky waters of Glasgow's tough underworld. In his spare time he prefers the clearer waters of the Tay near his home at Stanley.

He charts the decline of the salmon and offers his own explanation: 'This was a very prolific salmon river. The rods and nets lived in relative harmony for years. Then came the decline in white fishing at sea and the fishermen off the East Coast of Scotland started catching salmon, something which had traditionally been taboo. Previously you could not even mention the word "salmon" on a boat – it was considered bad luck and they were referred to as "red-fellows". But the fishermen began to realise that there was money to be made in illegally fishing for salmon. Recently it was discovered that the North-east of England Fishery, which operates legally, had increased its catch from a few thousand to 70 or 80,000. Until the 1960s, the migration of the salmon was something of a mystery but then a US submarine found them by chance under the ice of the Arctic. The Faroese and Greenland fishermen moved in and now they too will have to be bought off to conserve stocks. We also had a bad outbreak of disease among the fish and the growing number of seals gobble up thousands of salmon.

'All of this has had a bad effect on the river, especially at springtime. The Tay used to be noted as a spring river and anglers would come from all over Britain to fish in March, April and May. On some beats they would take 50 to 60 in a week. Now they are lucky to catch one. The Tay Salmon Fisheries Board, which controls the netting on the river, have made some attempts to increase the stocks and the lower tributaries have been seeded. Big runs of fish go up the Almond but thereafter there are very few. Huge runs of fish used to make their way up the river with the lower beats fishing in March, the middle beats in May and the upper beats in July. A sizeable run will go up the Ericht but after that only a few stragglers make it to the headwaters of the Tay.'

There are still a few visiting anglers prepared to pay £2,000 for a week's fishing on a prime Tay 'beat' but, like the salmon, they are becoming scarcer. A vital element of the Tay's economy is at stake. The salmon provide jobs for netters, ghillies, water bailiffs, the tourism trade and smokeries. In 1988 a survey by Perthshire's Tourist Board found that rod fishing on the Tay accounted for 350 jobs and contributed £5 million to the local economy. At last the threat is being taken seriously and a charitable organisation, the Tay Foundation, has been established to buy off the nets.

Mike Smith, a fishing proprietor/ghillie based at Dalguise, has campaigned for over a decade to improve the fishing on the river. A member of the Tay District Salmon Fishery Board, he is concerned that the right balance be struck in the use of the river, and that nature should be given a chance to replenish the salmon stocks. Although worried at the extent of drift-netting for salmon, he now sees grounds for optimism: 'The Government stance in allowing drift-netting is indefensible both nationally and internationally. Inshore drift-netting has been banned in Scotland since 1962 but it continues off the English north-east coast where huge numbers of salmon are being caught. But things are looking brighter. The Tay Foundation has raised £700,000 to buy off the upper estuary nets. That effectively allows 73,000 salmon and, more importantly, 70 million eggs into the river system. Thanks to the de-netting more fish have got up the river and high water has allowed a very good dispersal of the fish within the system. The fish counters at Pitlochry and on the Ericht have recorded increases.'

A reduction in netting has brought a welcome boost to the fish population but other pressures remain. Poaching is a lucrative, almost industrial activity, far removed in its use of poison for fishing and violence against water bailiffs, from the notion of one-for-the-pot in by-gone days. 'Wherever you get salmon,' says Mike, 'you get poaching. The problem is endemic on the Ericht around Blairgowrie and also at Perth Harbour during low water. The Tay Salmon Board employs ten water bailiffs to patrol the waters in a bid to stop the poachers.'

Mike highlights a new and growing problem for the Tay's hard-pressed salmon-fishers: 'I have warned the Perthshire Tourist Board about the increase in white-watersports. There has been a dramatic increase in canoeing and rafting on the river. There are now six different raft companies operating on its upper stretches. I know of an example where two English fishermen were taking a break to enjoy the tranquil surroundings of the river when 117 canoes and 11 inflatable dinghies came round the bend in the river. They just packed up and went home. That kind of abuse of the river plays havoc with the bird-life which nests by the banks, and spoils the fishing. It should be restricted to appropriate white-water stretches. They might claim that they leave no footprints but they are doing a lot of unseen damage. I feel that the value of rod fishing to the economy is consistently underestimated, and to preserve it we have to get the balance right in access to the river.'

For all of Mike's optimism, Arnott McWhinnie foresees a long, uphill battle before the river is restored to its former glory and he fears that, even if the decline in salmon numbers is reversed, access to the rivers for ordinary anglers will be restricted even further: 'The tide has turned in favour of the salmon but I don't think that the great days will ever come back in my lifetime. The salmon has a five-year life-cycle and it will take a long time to repair the damage. Strathtay is the most beautiful part of the river and should be a fisherman's paradise. A lot of anglers fear that if the riparian owners do invest money into restocking the river, they will pass the costs down the line and the fishing will become even more expensive. I personally feel that some kind of quota system should be introduced so that the river can become a resource to be used by everybody,'

Thousands of anglers still dream of catching a freshly-run Tay salmon and make an annual pilgrimage to fish the legendary beats and pools where, in 1922, Miss Georgina Ballantyne caught her 64 lb salmon which still stands as the British record. Some beats belong to much-criticised expensive time-share syndicates which may have paid up to £80,000 for a 99-year lease on a week's fishing. Others hire their sport from the hotels which line the river-bank. Few of the latter enjoy the proximity to the river of the luxurious Dunkeld House Hotel, built on the site of a former Atholl household, with two miles of fishing where the River Braan joins the Tay. The hotel's senior ghillie, Stan Pelc, is one of the hundred or so ghillies who work on the Tay and, at just 30 years of age, is one of the youngest. His domain comprises two beats and 16 named pools, among them Carrot Beds, Cutty Stone, Mousetrap, Cathedral Stream, Girnal, Ivy Tree and Fifey. Each will fish differently, depending on varying conditions, depth of water, flow of water, time of the year and, even, time of day. Stan's meticulous knowledge of his stretch is vital to the success of many visiting anglers: 'At the hotel's busiest times, I will work with 12 guests, six days a week. I would reckon we cater for around a thousand guests a year, fishing from both boats and the banks. Boat fishing is very much dependent on the height of the water. It needs to be about five feet above the summer level, so it is best on the Tay from 15 January to the end of April and from the end of August to the end of the season on 15 December. The method we use in the boats is called "harling" and is peculiar to the Tay. The boat works its way across a certain part of the river once the lengths and depths are set. We usually work our way down one of the pools. All the pools are good at certain times and I know their condition day in, day out. During the summer you can catch salmon from the bank but the best times are the first and last hours of the day.

The guests all have the same aim – to catch a salmon. As a keen fisherman who has fished the Tay for ten years, it's the same with me. In many ways, being a ghillie isn't like a job, it's a great therapy. The biggest salmon I have been involved with was 38½ lb and the biggest I have caught myself was 28 lb. Our busiest times are corporate days, when often some of the guests will have had no previous fishing experience, but it's surprising how many of them catch the bug.'

Apart from guiding guests, ghillies are also responsible for protecting the river from the ubiquitous poacher and for maintaining banks which have been eroded by spate and flood. 'The banks are constantly affected by the river,' says Stan. 'In the bad flood of 1990, we lost two boats and a hut. One of the boats was eventually found up a tree and we had to use a JCB to get it down. The Tay has a vast range of seasons in itself. If you can stick out springtime on this river, you can stick it out anywhere. But I definitely wouldn't move from here now. The river is my life. Being a ghillie is a fantastic way to live. I have travelled all over the world but there is nothing to rival a good day on the river.'

Unsuccessful anglers can at least console themselves by exploring some of Scotland's most beautiful scenery along the Tay and its tributaries. On the east bank, at Meikleour, famed for the world's largest beech hedge, the River Isla flows out of the Howe of Strathmore, a green swathe hemmed between the Sidlaws to the south and the Grampian mountains to the north. The Isla's current is swelled by the waters of the Ardle and Shee which tumble out of lovely Strathardle and majestic Glenshee before joining forces at Bridge of Cally. The fertile fields around Glamis Castle, the historic seat of the Strathmores and birth-place of Princess

Miss Georgina Ballantyne with her unequalled 64lb Tay salmon

Margaret, are drained by Dean Water which joins the Isla, fresh out of its Angus Glen, near the village of Meigle. The glens of Esk, Prosen, Clova, Isla and Shee cut through the Grampians like five great fingers, providing scenery more reminiscent of the West of Scotland in a corner of the country which is relatively undiscovered. The quiet market towns of Blairgowrie, Alyth, Kirriemuir, Forfar and Brechin sit at the mouths of their respective glens to cater for farming communities, visitors and the growing number of commuters.

From the west, the Almond runs parallel to the Earn to merge with the Tay above Perth, with Glenalmond offering a scenic route to Strathearn, Crieff, Comrie and, beyond, Loch Earn, the most southerly of the Tay's great lochs and a favourite haunt of weekend sailors and water-skiers. The Braan joins the Tay around 20 miles north of the Almond. It is one of the Tay's smaller tributaries and, as it thunders out of Strathbraan, crashing through a narrow gorge carved out of the surrounding woodland, it is one of the most beautiful. The area's natural beauty was enhanced by the Atholl family who created a tree garden here in the eighteenth century and built a summer-house known as Ossian's Hall or the Hermitage. Since 1943 the Hermitage and its 50 acres of forest have been in the care of the National Trust for Scotland and the beauty spot is regarded as a 'must' on the Tay tourist trail.

Scenery of quite a different sort – softer and greener – can be found just a few miles away on the road linking Dunkeld to Blairgowrie. When the glacier gouging out the Tay valley found itself obstructed at Birnam Pass, it spilled over a gap between Crieff Hill and Newtyle Hill to scrape out a hollow which has become a wildlife haven; it contains three lochs, all unusually rounded for this part of the world. Surrounded by semi-natural woodlands and marsh, the Loch of the Lowes, Loch of Craiglush and Butterstone Loch form a natural window on wildlife. In 1969 the Loch of the Lowes was taken over by the Scottish Wildlife Trust to form a nature reserve. Almost 90 per cent of its 98 hectares is under water and pride of place among the loch's vast array of bird, plant and mammal-life goes to the rare fish-eating ospreys who return to nest each summer, delighting thousands of visitors in the process.

The osprey died out in Scotland in 1916, having been hunted to extinction in the country by collectors who shot the birds and stole their eggs. A pair returned to Loch of Garten in the 1950s and the population began slowly to grow. Just weeks after the purchase of the Loch of Lowes by the Scottish Wildlife Trust, the ospreys gave the enterprise their seal of approval and appeared at the reserve. They have since become a symbol of the reserve. It was not until 1978 that a pair managed to breed successfully, but within four years 20 young ospreys had been reared at Lowes.

Alan Barclay, naturalist and ranger at the reserve since 1985, has the unenviable task of preserving the reserve's natural habitat and at the same time affording a curious public the opportunity to see the famous ospreys. 'A hide was constructed here in 1969 and three years later a visitor centre followed,' he says. 'The centre is really important because in 1991 there were 37,000 visitors to the reserve and we cannot do too many guided walks around the loch in the summer because it is vital to keep the area quiet for the ospreys. They are definitely the pulling factor for the crowds. They have been back here every single year since 1969 although they have not always hatched eggs. The birds arrive in April and, if they are breeding, leave in September. Two chicks were successfully hatched in 1991 and things are looking hopeful for more. One of the birds which returned this year was a chick that was reared here in 1982 – we are able to tell by the colour ringing we put on all chicks.

'The area around the Tay is a particularly suitable environment for ospreys. There is a

Dr Alan Barclay, Ranger at Loch of Lowes

diversity of habitats with food readily available in the river and the surrounding lochs. Ospreys will eat any kind of fish and the Loch of Lowes teems with pike and perch. The ospreys definitely give local people a pride in what is a very rich area for wildlife with over a hundred species of bird visiting the reserve, and two dozen different species of mammal resident – including wildcats which are not common. The main threat to a loch like this is obviously pollution. Chemicals can run off fields, and forestry can cause silting. But we are lucky as there is no real intensive farming around the loch. It has been kept as nature intended.'

Not all visitors to the reserve are well-disposed towards the birds and Alan and his team have to ensure round-the-clock security to beat egg thieves. Despite heavy fines and prison sentences these vandals continue to plague the nesting places of rare birds and pose a considerable menace to the osprey. 'It is estimated that one quarter to one third of osprey eggs are stolen every year,' stresses Alan. 'For a population of 70 pairs – not all of which will breed – that is a big threat. The problem is mainly confined to the eastern Highlands. There were several attempts in 1991 and we had to draft in the army! The Gordon Highlanders helped our

The Hermitage, Dunkeld

workers and volunteers to maintain a 24-hour watch during the five-week incubation period. Our hide is constantly manned during this time and we use night-sights and radio links to beat the thieves.'

There is, of course, much more to the wildlife of the reserve and of this stretch of the river than the ospreys. The volume and turbulence of the Tay ensures that the water is well oxygenated, making the river a giver of life to a myriad of insects, which in turn encourages bird-life. The shingle banks of the river provide a fascinating habitat for naturalists and National Trust for Scotland rangers work with schoolchildren to help them discover the wildlife lurking under the stones and boulders studded with semi-precious garnets in the river-bed.

As well as enchanting visitors and tourists, the superb countryside in this part of Perthshire exercises a powerful pull on locals who venture further afield to make their living. When they can, many return to the area to work or retire. Scots singer-songwriter Dougie Maclean is a good example. He lives at the old schoolhouse at Butterstone and the school building where he and his father were educated now houses Dougie's recording studio. Perhaps best known for *Caledonia*, a pop song which has become a modern nationalist anthem on the familiar theme of exile and return, Dougie has also found inspiration in these tranquil surroundings to pen a song which was selected by Twentieth-Century Fox for inclusion in their film, *The Last of the Mohicans*.

Dougie's career has taken him to both Europe and North America, where he still tours and distributes records and CDs under his Dunkeld label. But for Dougie it is a case of 'east or west, home is best' and he has eschewed commercial considerations to remain close to his heritage and the hills of home.

'My grandfather was a local shepherd and he took me up all the hills where I discovered many of the Pictish stones and burial sites that are littered around the area,' he explains. 'When I was a teenager, I honestly could not wait to get out and I spent many years working abroad in Europe. I eventually moved back to Butterstone because I love it and missed it so much. I think it is very important that communities like ours should be lived in by local people and not be full of retired people or holiday homes. When local people stay in a place it means that the songs, stories, traditions and culture live on. That gives an area a life and vibrancy which is very different from the picture most tourists see. I think that more people should realise how important it is to stay in their local area and promote its culture – otherwise there is a real danger that many towns and villages will become tourist ghost towns which only have any sense of life about them for two months of the year.

'Most of my songs are inspired by the countryside and the area around the Tay. *Caledonia* was written in France and was inspired by my wanting to get back here. Growing up in the countryside around the Tay has added real depth of feeling to my songs. Having a stable home

Singer-songwriter, Dougie Maclean

base here helps put things into perspective. In my songs I try to create something which is distinctively Scottish and not kitsch. For me, an area and its culture has to have something real about it. I am unimpressed by the tartanry created by the Victorians.'

Dougie's plea for the hamlets of the Tay to retain their own identity and local population is endorsed by folk along the river. Lack of work, the spiralling cost of housing inflated by the arrival of incoming 'white settlers', and the freeze on construction of new council housing, however, conspire to encourage locals to leave the area. Yet, historic Dunkeld has successfully met the challenge of keeping its character and satisfying the annual influx of tourists.

A cradle of Christianity in Scotland, Dunkeld has been host to a Christian institution since the first Christian settlement in the sixth century. An abbey was founded in 815 when monks from Iona took refuge in the heart of Scotland from marauding Vikings. The monks brought Iona's ancient books and relics with them for safekeeping. In 844 Kenneth Macalpin declared Dunkeld and Scone twin capitals in the new kingdom he forged by uniting the Picts and the Scots. Just one year later, the peace of this Highland sanctuary was shattered when the Danes fought their way up the Tay valley to plunder the ancient town and its monastery. They came back in 905 to destroy four decades of hard labour which had been put into rebuilding Dunkeld. Despite their defeat by the Scots at Luncarty, the Danes returned in 1027 to destroy Dunkeld for the third time. The town was put to the torch for the final time in 1689 when an army of 5,000 Highlanders rose in support of the dethroned Stewart king, James VII. Led by Grahame of Claverhouse, the legendary strategist who entered Scottish folklore as 'Bonnie Dundee', the Highlanders defeated Government forces in the famous Battle of Killiecrankie on the banks of the River Garry – although not without the loss of their leader. Deprived of Dundee's military know-how the Highlanders cornered a force of 1,200 Cameronians in the centre of Dunkeld but lost their advantage when the besieged Cameronians used the cover of darkness to lock the rebel troops in the houses they had occupied and then burnt them alive. Only three houses and the battle-scarred cathedral remained standing. The appalling consequences spelt the end of what had been a minor civil war, but it was not to be the last time that Highland blood was shed for the Stuart cause.

Dunkeld and its sister village of Birnam across the Tay are among the river's most charming communities. Both enjoy a huge natural advantage in their majestic setting in an amphitheatre chiselled out of the rugged hills which announce the traveller's entry to the Highlands. These tree-clad slopes can offer a Gothic spectacle in winter when the mist clinging to their contours slowly lifts, and they provide a marvellous, richly coloured embroidery in autumn, a sure sign that the area has avoided the fate of so much of the Highlands which have disappeared under a uniform blanket of the alien Sitka spruce. In fact, this forest of fir, oak, ash, birch and beech is not as natural as it might appear. During the eighteenth century it was here that the larch was first introduced into Britain from the Tyrol, and in the last century the Duke of Atholl ordered canisters of mixed seed to be fired from cannon at the precipitous slopes to give nature a helping hand in clothing barren rocky outcrops.

This is the landscape – more Highland in nature – which inspired the imaginations of Wordsworth, Burns, Gray, Scott and even, in the case of *Macbeth*, Shakespeare. Here too, at her family's holiday home in Birnam, Beatrix Potter discovered the magic of the Perthshire countryside. It is commonly believed that the 'Peter Rabbit' tales were inspired by her beloved Lake District but, in fact, it was the scenery and animal life around the Tay that entranced her.

Every summer for 12 years the Potter family travelled from London to spend their holidays by the Tay. 'I do not remember a time when I did not make for myself a fairyland amongst the wild flowers, the animals, funghi, mosses, woods and streams; all the thousand objects of the countryside,' she wrote of these happy days.

In 1893 Beatrix penned an amusing picture-letter to a friend which later became the basis of *The Tale of Peter Rabbit*; almost one hundred years later it sold at auction for £82,500. Her three-month summer stays also inspired her to create characters like Mrs Tiggywinkle, based on a Dunkeld washerwoman, and Mr Jeremy Fisher, modelled on an angling friend of the author's father, which have delighted generations of small children. A garden has now been established in Birnam to commemorate one of the Tay's least-known literary connections. The Beatrix Potter Garden and Exhibition Centre has recreated the fantasy world of Peter Rabbit. Footpaths lead past the homes of Mr Tod and Mrs Tiggywinkle and alongside the stream and pond where Mr Jeremy Fisher lives to reach Peter Rabbit's burrow. The centre also boasts an exhibition which focuses on Beatrix's scientific and personal links with the area.

Caputh Ferry, 1903

The people of Dunkeld and Birnam cherish their heritage, and an active local history society with 80 members digs away, researching the area's past to publish little pamphlets which have become indispensable to historians, amateur and professional alike. Chairperson of the Dunkeld and Birnam Historical Society is Eileen Cox who, married to a descendant of the famous Dundee jute dynasty, now bears a name inextricably linked with the modern history of the Tay.

She lives at Blackhill, on the corner of Snaigow estate just outside Dunkeld which was owned by William Cox, one of the greatest of Tayside's jute barons: 'My husband William is the great-grandson of William Cox. In the latter years of the jute boom, many of the members of the Cox family acquired country estates. The house at Snaigow is the last corner of the estate which we own. In its heyday it was a large working estate. I am very interested in history, having completed a history degree at St Andrews, where I met my husband. I am researching the history of the Cox family at the moment and am trying to go back as early as I can. They were definitely among the first business entrepreneurs and were really self-made men. I think that the jute barons have been maligned by popular history. At the height of their powers they did a lot for Dundee, not just in terms of employment but in providing schools, parks and housing.

'I have been very interested in researching the history of Caputh parish. I am slowly collating all the people who have made up its population starting from records in 1650. It is a slow process but it shows that the parish has a rich tradition. Our family has an interesting connection with the village in that William and his brother James were instrumental in the construction of the railway bridge across the Tay. James was the Lord Provost of Dundee and helped by securing some of the old girders from the original Tay rail bridge for inclusion in the bridge at Caputh. He was heavily involved in raising the finance for the first bridge and I don't think that he ever got over the fact that it fell down.'

The next project for members of the historical society will be to research and publish a history of Dunkeld Cathedral. A mixture of Gothic and Norman architecture, the cathedral was successively added to by different bishops over the centuries. A part of the building is still used for worship but the edifice and its smooth lawns which sweep down to the river are now largely a visitor attraction. Among its more gruesome sights is the Leper's Peep, a chink in the outer wall near the pulpit which allowed lepers to receive the sacrament without coming into contact with the rest of the congregation.

Maintenance of this ancient structure is a vital and skilled job and Ian Sinclair, stone-mason on the cathedral, has become an expert on the history of his charge. 'I've lived all of my days in Birnam and now stay in a cottage on what was part of the Atholl estate. It dates back to the building of the bridge over the Tay in 1809. I served my time locally and have been working on the cathedral for over a decade. I would say that I know every nook and cranny of it now. It is quite a good job, and we have to make sure that the building is maintained in a reasonable condition.

'The Reformation caused a tremendous amount of damage to the cathedral and the Battle of Dunkeld in 1689 did not do it much good either. In defending the village, the Cameronians led by Colonel Clelland ran out of shot and the lead from the cathedral roof was taken down and melted. This was an important battle because it set back the Jacobite cause. Colonel Clelland is buried here and in recent years some people have come and had a service at his grave. We found a mass grave a few years ago when we were putting in a new drain. It was quite shocking to find all those skeletons. So many of them had wounds to the skull, a sure sign of a hard-fought

Ian Sinclair, stonemason at Dunkeld Cathedral

battle. Another possible connection with the Jacobites emerged a few years ago when a chap arrived claiming that Bonnie Prince Charlie's grandson was buried at the cathedral. We found the grave of a General Charles Edward Stuart, known as Count Rhenstart, who died after a coach accident in 1854. The dates fit but we cannot be sure. But I would like to think it is true.'

Working on the cathedral has enabled Ian to become something of an archaeologist. He explains, 'Many of the graves in the Cathedral are of servants of the Atholl family. They had a house on the Tay on the present site of Dunkeld House Hotel. A lot of the walks by the Tay were private Atholl tracks at one time and the Atholl family still own the land the Cathedral is built on. Once, while working on the top of the tower, my predecessor and I noticed strange lines in a field that had been cropped by a farmer. The lines and circle loooked like an old garden of some sort. A chap who was divining in the area came down one day and told us that he had found lots of tracks and foundations. We also found a stone by the edge of the river that might have been part of a bridge of some sort. I know that the old road to the cathedral followed that path, so it makes sense for a bridge to have been there. It was probably constructed by the monks.

'It is a very satisfying job. The important thing is that when I am dead and gone, I've helped to keep something that has been around for centuries and will hopefully be so for many more. I enjoy the tourists when they come and like to have a bit of fun with them, I tell them that I am a descendant of Bishop Sinclair who was here hundreds of years ago and show them his grave. I tell the doubters that the motto of the Clan Sinclair is "Commit Thy Works To God" and insist that it is destiny that I ended up here. The Yanks seem to like it and I get my picture taken a lot.'

Ian's frequent references to the powerful Atholl family are a reminder of the days when their feudal writ ran large in the area. Indeed, a few miles north at Blair Atholl the current duke still exercises his right, now ceremonial, to muster Britain's only authorised private army, the Atholl Highlanders. The relationship between the laird and the lowly was not always one of benevolent paternalism, however, and on occasion there was dissent from the latter. Telford's splendid bridge across the Tay, which can best be seen from the cathedral, provided the stage for a remarkable outbreak of civil disobedience which resulted in Dunkeld briefly being subject to martial law and the eventual abolition of toll bridges in Britain.

The bridge was built in 1809, partly funded by the Government and partly by the fourth Duke of Atholl who was given the right to recover his investment by raising tolls. He died in 1828 but the right to raise the tolls was inherited by his successors. As the years passed and details of the bridge accounts and the balance due became foggier, suspicions on the part of local people grew. The arrival of the Perth to Inverness railway at Birnam fuelled the discontent with passengers alighting for Dunkeld irate at having to pay the bridge toll on top of their fare. The spark which finally ignited the Dunkeld Toll Riots was the arrogant refusal of the Duke of Atholl to receive a deputation from the Free Church of Dunkeld in 1867. Many of the Free Kirk's members resided in Birnam and poor, often large, families could not afford to pay bridge tolls for each family member as well as contribute to church collections.

Under cover of darkness a group of protesters locked the toll-keeper in his house – which can still be seen on the bridge – and hurled the gates into the Tay. When they were reinstated within 24 hours, a crowd of 500 assembled and, armed with axes, destroyed the gates, fencing, gate-keeper's box and signboards. The police were prevented from arresting the ringleaders and the rioters triumphantly paraded through the streets of Dunkeld brandishing their trophies from the wrecked tolls. The arrival of police reinforcements backed up by a detachment of the Black Watch did little to intimidate the villagers who turned out *en masse*, and, led by a brass band and a piper, paraded through the area including the 'free' bridge on their route. After a long legal wrangle the amount of debt claimed by the Duke of Atholl was eventually reduced from £55,000 to £16,000. Such was the sensitivity surrounding the gates that when they were finally removed in May 1879, council workmen took them down at the dead of night to avoid jubilant demonstrations.

Dunkeld has changed little since those heady days of popular protest. The centre of the town, crouched around the market cross so typical of villages on the Tay, has been lovingly restored, mainly thanks to the efforts of the National Trust for Scotland which has restored the 'Little Houses' in Cathedral Street and runs the 'Ell Shop' in the square. Gillian Kelly, the resident National Trust for Scotland representative, takes up the story: 'The "Little Houses" date back to the rebuilding of Dunkeld after 1689 and are an important part of the town's heritage. Originally part of the Atholl estates, they are situated at the market cross and Cathedral Street. The Trust became involved in the 1950s. At that time the 40 houses and two shops were condemned and were offered to the Trust without an endowment. But Perth County Council agreed to take on half the houses and the scheme was born from there. The Trust looked at the scheme as a long-term project, and an important element was that the houses should be occupied by local people, meaning that the houses are still a part of a living local community.'

The Ell shop, selling local crafts and souvenirs, is named after an early measure for regulating lengths of cloth. Gillian elaborates, 'We have an ell fixed to the side of the shop. It dates from 1706 and was an early example of weights and measures control. It was used in the marketplace and weavers could check their rods against it. The marketplace was of enormous importance to the local community and now the shop and houses are important to the economy of the town. It is a good example of vernacular restoration at its best.'

The market square at Dunkeld is also host to one of the Tay's more unusual military institutions. The Scottish Horse Regimental Museum commemorates a regiment raised during the Boer War by the Caledonian Society of Johannesburg. Recruitment in Scotland was aided by the Duke of Atholl, who drew from the area's ghillies and stalkers to forge a tough regiment of sharp-shooters capable of tackling the Boers in guerrilla warfare. The regiment went on to serve in both World Wars, seeing action at Gallipoli and Normandy. Between the wars, volunteers attended the annual camp at Blair Atholl, bringing their own horses with them just as their forefather clansmen would have done.

The gamekeepers and stalkers of the Tay still have a link with Dunkeld in the only slightly less martial shape of Major Neil Ramsay. He runs one of the country's most important sporting agencies for hunters who travel to Scotland's grouse moors and deer forests for the famed quality of the shooting. From his office in Dunkeld, just 50 yards from the Tay, he controls an operation which arranges packages for up to 500 visitors each year. They come from countries as wide-ranging as Lebanon, South Africa, New Zealand, Australia, Argentina, the United States and Venezuela.

Shooting-parties are a vital component of the Highland economy, providing a lifeline for many estates in what is one of Europe's last great tracts of wilderness. A Government report has estimated that commercial field sports are worth about £80 million and that grouse-shooting

Dunkeld street scene

alone accounts for £26 million. The grouse moors of Perthshire around the Tay have an allure all of their own for visitors.

'When the railways opened up the Highlands in the last century, a great number of sporting lodges were built,' Major Ramsay elaborates. 'In many ways the economy of the Highlands was carried on the back of grouse and there is still a ring of truth to that today. People are fascinated by the bird. There are very few grouse moors in Tayside which do not cater for visiting shooting-parties and there is no doubt that grouse-shooting provides many part-time and full-time jobs. Estates now look upon paying shooters as important for their upkeep. Some are more commercial than others and the larger estates tend to have bigger operations.'

The world of the professional sporting agent is now fiercely competitive and business-like. 'When it comes to arranging package deals we are very flexible and can put as much or as little as the visitor wants into it', explains Major Ramsay. 'I can arrange everything for them, including transport to and from airports, hotels, insurance and documentation for weapons. We liaise closely with the estates and I am so busy in the office and meeting all the parties that I don't really have time to shoot with them. Some weeks there are 16 to 20 parties in the country and getting around them all does not leave me a lot of time for shooting.'

As with so many of the people who live by the Tay, he has succeeded in transforming a hobby into a full-time job – the dream of countless thousands trapped in the urban rat race. 'I

The River Tay from Dunkeld Cathedral

have lived around the Tay for 60 years,' he smiles. 'My father lived in Aberfeldy and he had shooting parties on his own moor. I myself started taking people to shoot with me at Aberfeldy in 1960. More and more people wanted to go shooting and it has grown into a business across the country.'

Chapter VI

THE HEART OF SCOTLAND

Upstream from Dunkeld the Tay Valley widens as the river arcs round in a graceful sweep to its source in the mountains of the west. The mood of the river on this stretch is mercurial: the flow changes suddenly from a sure, dark certainty to a frivolous shimmering dance across broad shingle banks, only to transform itself again into an angry torrent bouncing and crashing over the giant boulders of its white-water rapids. Just as it emerges from its Highland glen at the hamlet of Logierait the Tay is joined by the Tummel, one of the great river's most beautiful tributaries. The valley etched out by the Tummel carries the main road and rail routes north to Pitlochry, the lands of Atholl and Inverness beyond.

In a mere 20 miles, the Tummel flows through a series of three mighty lochs. Rannoch, Tummel and the man-made Faskally provide some of Highland Perthshire's most fantastic scenery, earning one vista the title of 'Queen's View'. Situated at the eastern end of Loch Tummel, it lies in Allean Forest, one of the Tay Forest Park's six forest walking areas. Three walks have been laid out in Allean to allow visitors to experience a varied terrain clad with a canopy of spruce, pine, larch and Douglas Fir, and carpeted with a mottled blue-brown mixture of Scottish bluebells and bracken. The trail also affords walkers a glimpse of life in by-gone times at archaeological sites which include a restored eighteenth-century farmstead, the remains of an eighth-century ring fort, and neolithic standing stones.

Walking is the best way to see the sights and the only way to savour the smells and sounds of the countryside on this stretch of the Tay river system. The Forestry Commission has opened up the Tay Forest Park to visitors, made parking easy and designed a number of short, non-challenging walks. The National Trust has done the same at the Linn of Tummel, at Craigower near Pitlochry and at the famed Pass of Killiecrankie. The last-named is on the River Garry, which joins the Tummel at Faskally and reaches north to Blair Atholl and historic Blair Castle, home to the Dukes of Atholl and a memorable visit on any itinerary.

For naturalists and ornitholigists the habitat around the Highland Tay is a paradise and even dyed-in-the-wool 'townies' cannot but be impressed by the fantastic range of flora and fauna in this huge natural park. The huge Capercaillie, once extinct in Britain, was reintroduced to this part of Perthshire in 1837 and is now the symbol of the Tay Forest Park. Weighing in at 17 lb, the Capercaillie is one of Scotland's largest birds, but these same forests also harbour the tiny Goldcrest, the rare Black Grouse, native Scottish Crossbill, Tree Pipits,

Spotted Flycatchers and a growing population of birds of prey. Leaving behind the flat, lush green plains which celebrate the Tay's confluence with the Tummel, the hills close in, protective of an infant Tay screened now by a rich curtain of oak, beech, hazel, ash, sycamore and rowan. The hilly farming land on both sides of the glen is embellished with emerald and opal forests tinged with deciduous amber.

Forestry is indeed a semi-precious business for many families who rely on it for a living in this part of Tayside. Surveying the luxuriant green swathes which cloak the hills, it is difficult to imagine how this must have looked 200 years ago when deforestation had left in its wake a bleak and barren landscape, prompting Dr Johnson to remark during his famous tour of Scotland in 1773 that 'a tree in Scotland was as rare as a horse in Venice'.

From its base in Dunkeld the Forestry Commission, also known as Forest Enterprise, employs around 130 people. Charlie Taylor is the district forest manager for Tay Forest Park and has responsibility for striking a balance between the demands of conservation and commerce, public access and the demands of forestry operational works. 'We manage all the state-run forests throughout the whole of Tayside. The entire Tayside area is planned from the Dunkeld office. Half of the forest is designated as the Tay Forest Park and within that there are special designated areas of high recreational value. In the environs of the River Tay there are approximately 20,000 acres of a whole range of trees. The area has a long history of forest management. In many ways, it is the cradle of Scottish forestry. The Dukes of Atholl in the eighteenth century replanted bare hills around Dunkeld with larch imported from Europe. It is one of the best tree-growing areas in Scotland. It has a mild climate with good old brown earth in which the trees can get good roots. This allows us to plan some areas up to 500 years in advance while others are on shorter rotation. The area around the Tay here is as good as you get for forestry.

'Craigvinean, above Dalguise on the east bank of the river, is where the Atholls began planting. They were doing it for their private gain but we are managing it for the public, with mountain bike trails, walks and the like. The Dunkeld area is a natural scenic area. The largest proportion of forest is taken up by conifers and they are well managed and look attractive. The current forest is predominantly spruce.

'Good management and time are the keys to good forestry. The Tay forms a valley and on the lower slopes and sides it is more sheltered and thus better for tree-growing. I am in overall control of the state forests in the district and my role is concerned with strategy, deciding what to fell and what to plant. I set up the structure. One of the aspects that appeals about the job is the sense of history – it's nice to feel that you are involved in something that will last. This is probably one of the best areas in Scotland to work. There are a lot of things to do, and it is reasonably sheltered so we can hold events for that bit longer and grow things longer too. I am originally from Fort William and here I feel as if I am working in the tropical south. I had always wanted to work in this area as it has such a large range of opportunities.'

Over 200,000 visitors each year take advantage of the walks and amenities offered by Forest Enterprise, which has to be congratulated on its initiative in opening up the Tay Forest Park. Although the forests are more accessible than ever, forestry has become a highly controversial topic in recent years. Fittingly for an area described by Charlie as 'the cradle of Scottish forestry', it is home to the Scottish Native Woods Campaign, an environmentalist group fighting to protect and extend what little remains of the native Scottish forest.

In his Aberfeldy office, Alan Drever, the director of the campaign, explains; 'The native woodlands of Scotland are part of a heritage which goes back 8,000 years to just after the Ice Age. Three-quarters of Scotland was covered in natural woodland at this time. There was a distinction between the Highlands and Lowlands with oak produced in the latter and pine and birch in the former. That has now been reduced to just 1 per cent of the land area in Scotland and nine-tenths of that 1 per cent is in the Highlands, all that is left of the Caledonian pine forest.'

Alan points to countries like Finland where 40 per cent of the country is covered in native woodland and passionately believes that the destruction of Scottish native woodland has been to the detriment of the the ecological value of a part of Scotland's heritage which, as he says, 'is as important to Scotland as Edinburgh Castle'.

He charts the eclipse of Scotland's native woods: 'The Highland native forest has really declined sharply since the 1700s, due to improved communications and the exploitation of pine for military use. A further blow came in the 1800s with the introduction of sheep into the large Highland estates after the clearances. Pine and birch usually regenerate fairly quickly, but they were not given a chance by sheep, which ate everything in their path, including seedlings. The sheep over-grazed, which was not part of the natural woodland life-cycle.'

Alan believes that the steps taken in this century to remedy deforestation have been too inflexible and commercially orientated. 'I believe that the Forestry Commission, established in 1919, ignored the native woodland as a resource,' he states. 'What we now have is tree-farming where the Sitka spruce is the name of the game. These processes destroy the natural woodlands and there was also a great deal of underplanting. I was born in 1950 and during my lifetime a third of Scotland's natural woodland has disappeared. It must be confusing for people who travel by the Tay. They see the vast number of trees around the valley but these are mainly Sitka spruce and not native to this country.'

The Scottish Community Woods Campaign was established in 1988 and has filled an important gap in forestry conservation. The charity has television naturalist David Bellamy as a patron, and works with farmers and landowners to explain the value of native woodlands as Scotland's best and richest source of wildlife. It has also organised a 'Growing Up With Trees' project involving 70 Perthshire schools which encourages children to grow native trees from seed.

Alan stresses the importance of maintaining the native genetic strain of woodland: 'There is a diverse variety of plant and animal-life in native woodlands because of the 8,000-year chain of evolution present in them. Different insects have evolved which are closely integrated with native trees and their leaves; the birch for example has over 200 species of insect associated with it. The invasion of non-native trees has inhibited this rich life in certain respects. It is important that the seeds we use for the children's projects are all local. They will have an 8,000-year pedigree stretching back to the first local forest, so genetically we will be able to fit in perfectly. This pedigree relates to climate and rainfall, so a West Highland seed would not have the pedigree to fit into East Highland soil.

'Surveys conducted by the Nature Conservancy Council among others estimate that 96 per cent of the seed stock sold in Scottish nurseries is not Scottish, and that 50 per cent is not even British. This means that the crucial genetic base of our woodlands is being diluted and that the resistance of the native trees has been reduced, a worrying factor with the advent of acid rain. The birches around Aberfeldy have an 8,000-year blood-line; they are a living history and also of great value to the landscape, which is very important for tourism. I have no doubt that birch woodland is a favourite for many people. The trees are a very attractive colour and have an appealing delicate shape. The famous Birks o' Aberfeldy are situated in a gorge valley which is rich and natural. This steepness means that there has never been grazing and so a very good natural example of woodland has been preserved.'

Charlie Taylor is not without sympathy for Alan's beliefs but he makes a plea for a middle road; 'We do plant native trees and I believe that there is room for everything. We certainly look after native forests like the Blackwood of Rannoch, a surviving part of the old Caledonian Forest. We see an opportunity for everything. But we cannot lose sight of economic factors. Britain still imports 90 per cent of its timber. In the past there was a policy of growing conifers for quick productions to reduce timber imports. A lot of forests were cut down 200 years ago and we have to grow more trees.

'There has to be a range. Native oak and pine look good and are attractive but we need productive conifers too. It is a question of balance and it has to be sensitively managed. You have to be careful things don't swing too far towards single-objective forestry. Native woodlands are important, but so are conifers.'

The integration of forestry with tourism has come as a boon to an area which has welcomed visitors for over a hundred years, since the Victorians, led by Queen Victoria herself, discovered the joys of the Perthshire countryside. The arrival in the 1860s of the railway in the Tay's Highland glen opened the area up for development. A station was opened at Grandtully, behind the present Grandtully Hotel, and wealthy Victorians built superb Scots baronial-style granite homes. Many of these are tucked away in the woods around the village of Strathtay, just across the narrow iron-girder bridge which incorporates a memorial to one of those early tourists, Charles Brockbank of Birmingham, who drowned at this spot in 1873.

The bridge is a good vantage point to view Grandtully White Water where the Tay's spectacular rapids provide Britain's best stretch of natural slalom and white-water canoeing. The Scottish Canoe Association runs several major events with up to 250 competitors taking part, and canoeists are on this part of the river virtually all year round. Raft companies operating from the Fradle Rock tea-room at Grandtully offer trips down the river which afford visitors a unique perspective from which to view the scenery and wildlife of the Tay.

Strathtay has been a village in decline for the last three decades, mirroring the decline of farming and the drift of locals from the land. The village still supports a nine-hole golf course but where there were once half a dozen shops, there is now only one, a general store which incorporates the local post office. Yet this was once a thriving parish and the fine granite war memorial at the end of the bridge records the loss of 21 Strathtay men in the First World War and a further nine killed in the Second World War.

The five-mile-long narrow and winding road from Strathtay to Weem and Aberfeldy hugs the north bank of the river. On the hills above the road the Victorians carved out seven great sporting estates and one of these, Cluny House, now has gardens open to the public. The garden was developed from a field as recently as 1950 by its owner, Robert Masterton, the local vet, and is lovingly managed today by his daughter and son-in-law. The approach to the five-acre garden is guarded by two giant Wellingtonia, one of them with a girth of 35.5 feet. The garden is well known for its collection of Himalayan, Tibetan, North American and Japanese plants which has been put together over the years by its creators. Close by is Tombuie Farm where the Crystal family have turned over some of the land to deer farming with a herd of a hundred hinds with calves and some magnificent stags. The farm is part of the Environmentally Sensitive Scheme of the Breadalbane area, which is funded by the European

Community to encourage farmers to maintain the countryside in its original form. In 1991 Donald and Sally Crystal, whose family have farmed Tombuie since the 1940s, opened a smokehouse in a further effort to diversify. The art of cheese-making, once common on the farms of this area, has been revived and the final product can be purchased at the farm.

Across the river is Aberfeldy, the last of the Tay's large settlements and a village steeped in history. Aberfeldy is entered from the north bank of the river by crossing General Wade's famous bridge, built in 1733 and at one time the only bridge across the Tay. The five-arched bridge was designed by William Adam, the father of the renowned architect Robert Adam, and was an integral part of the military road network constructed by the Hanoverian general between 1725 and 1740. The bridge was something of an architectural triumph in its day; now, just a few hundred yards downstream, is another civil engineering first for Scotland: the newest bridge to span the Tay it is also the river's most unusual. A pedestrian crossing linking Aberfeldy's golf course with the north bank of the river, it is the world's first fibreglass bridge. Built by a pioneering team of civil engineers from Dundee University, it was completed in 1992 and has attracted international attention for a process which could revolutionise bridge-building and design. The bridge, two metres wide and 62 metres long, is the world's first large-scale bridge to be made wholly out of fibreglass reinforced plastic, a material which gives considerable strength but which is so light-weight that no cranes were needed in its construction.

Sadly, Aberfeldy has not made the kind of graceful transition which has allowed Dunkeld to retain its character as a working village and at the same time accommodate the needs of tourists. Aberfeldy's main street is a trifle dowdy and sometimes too brash but, against that, local people have devised Locus, an award-winning tourism scheme which is sensitive to the people, history, landscape and wildlife of the locality and which aims to develop positive relationships between visitors and residents.

Aberfeldy's distillery, a part of the United Distillers group, is a good example of how a working unit can also satisfy tourist demand. Just over 20 local folk are employed at the distillery which contributes its distinctive spirit to some of the world's best-known blends, Johnny Walker, White Horse, Vat 69 and Dewar's among them. In recent years the distillery has developed its own Highland malt and now welcomes visitors.

'There is a great pride in the community in Aberfeldy and visitors have often remarked to me about this,' explains manager Brian Bisset. 'It is important that visitors get a chance to see what makes the community work. Distilling has always been a part of Aberfeldy and local tradesmen are used to this day. Two hundred years ago there were a large number of distilleries around Aberfeldy, many of them illegal, but now this is the last distillery left on the Tay. It was established in 1896 and production started in 1898. It was built by the sons of John Dewar, the founder of the whisky empire who was born the son of a crofter about two miles from Aberfeldy and who died in 1880 by the banks of the Tay.

'The site that was chosen is near the Pitilie Burn, which is a tributary of the Tay and an excellent source of clean, pure water as it flows down into the river. The quality of the water had earlier supported the Pitilie distillery, which ceased production in 1850. That is why this site was chosen by Dewar's and the water rights were acquired from the Marquis of Breadalbane. It is important that the water comes from above the farms. Water for the distillery is still drawn from the ruins of the Pitilie Distillery as the water is sufficiently pure for distilling.

Canoeing on Grandtully white water

Brian Bisset, manager of the Aberfeldy Distillery

Douglas Wilson, miller at Aberfeldy Meal Mill

'We make the unique Aberfeldy single malt whisky here. It is 15 years old, 43 per cent proof and classed as a Highland whisky. Its character comes from its heavily peated nature – but that is something which is not done deliberately. It is a light malt whisky which is very easily accepted by the palate. I think it reflects the beauty of the surrounding countryside. The logo on the label is of the red squirrel which can be seen in the woods of the surrounding countryside. We have acquired some nearby oak woodland, have begun planting trees for the squirrels and are thinking about a nature trail, which will be a very long-term project. The countryside beside the Tay is rich in wild life and we try to encourage it. I estimate there were over 30 species of bird nesting around here. Roe deer live in the wood and there is also a tawny owl which nests. It makes the area ideal to work in and we have put up nest boxes to encourage the wildlife.'

Distilling is not the only trade dependent on the river and its farming community to become a tourist attraction in its own right. Aberfeldy originally developed as a community centred around the mills powered by the Moness Burn and which were built to cut wood and process meal, lint and wool. A tweed mill still survives and in 1987 the Aberfeldy Meal Mill, built in 1826, was restored and opened to visitors.

Douglas Wilson, Aberfeldy's only miller, supervises an environmentally-aware operation which is capable of processing three tons of oats a day. In the health-conscious 1990s the mill sells its products direct to the public and has become a welcome addition to Aberfeldy's tourist trail. He explains the age-old process of which he is guardian: 'My job involves the complete process of turning oats, fresh from the farm, into meal. When they come in, the oats are dried to reduce the moisture to 10 per cent. They are then put into the kiln drier which takes them down to 4 per cent moisture. The next step is the shelling process which takes the oat down to the groat and they are then ground down. It may sound simple but the oats go through a series of chutes and escalators, around the three-storey building, before they make it into the packet.

'We sell meal here and also to healthfood stores. The waste products such as shells and dust are taken to the Burnside Mill in Cupar, Fife, where they are made into animal feed, so that nothing goes to waste. The water-wheel is powered by the Moness Burn, which is a tributary of the Tay. The wheel only needs about an inch of water flowing to get it turning and we can control the flow with the aid of a trapdoor. The mill was still used in the early 1970s, but it was in ruins and made only animal foodstuffs.'

Douglas is a keen advocate of the eco-friendly aspects of water-milling: 'Working at the water mill really opens your eyes to the power that can be taken from the natural environment without actually damaging the planet. It is a very efficient way of making oatmeal – the power for the stones is free so there are no overheads in that respect. If we go hard we could shell and grind three tons of oatmeal per day. It isn't too physically demanding because there are machines to lift the sacks. The space in here means that we couldn't do much more than three tons. The grinding stones are made of sandstone but have a French burr face on them which is the top of the range for this sort of stone. The water wheel is 15 feet in diameter and can achieve a power of around 10 to 15 horsepower.'

As he explains, milling is a way of life which has come to suit his personal approach to life: 'I was asked in about ten years ago to help with the kiln and I just stayed. I am originally from East Kilbride and moved here to get out of the rat-race. I formerly worked as a lab technician for the Clyde River Water Authority and, compared to that, the waters of the Tay are so pure and clean. I worked at tree-planting when I first came to Aberfeldy and I would say that the countryside around here is unrivalled in Scotland. I believe that there were seven mills around Aberfeldy at one time, so water has always played a major part of the local economy. The big mills served all the farms in the area. Milling is a very honest trade and there is no modern technology. It is easy to fix things when they break down because all of the parts are easy to see. It is very 'hands on' work and you can increase the efficiency enormously when you adjust the machinery.

'The oats that are milled at the Aberfeldy water-mill are local and 100 per cent organic. Trade is definitely picking up because of increased environmental awareness in society. There are absolutely no additives in the oatmeal which is sold here. Ninety per cent of the visitors who come here usually buy a bag of oatmeal. It can be ground as fine, medium or coarse. There are no instructions on the packet but I couldn't imagine anybody going very far wrong with it.'

The miller's words are sweet music to Dr Walter Yellowlees, the retired and much respected former general practitioner for Aberfeldy, who, like A. J. Cronin's 'Dr Finlay', arrived in a Highland practice just after the last war to help out an older colleague. Originally from Paisley, Dr Yellowlees served in the army for four years after graduating from Edinburgh University. He arrived at Aberfeldy in 1948, his first rural practice, and has remained ever since. His outsider's eye alerted him to a startling fact. He recalls, 'My worries were prompted when I found that, despite the beautiful peace, scenery and slow tempo of life in Aberfeldy, health was not improved as a result. The farmers, foresters and game-keepers I treated did not suffer from lack of exercise or live in an unhealthy environment, but they succumbed to coronaries, cancers and diabetes just the same as those in urban areas. The problem was not just confined to cities.'

Dr Yellowlees' conclusions then were seen as 'crankish'. Today they are casually and widely accepted. He concluded that diet was a critical factor in impairing health and advocated a high-fibre diet with a reduction in refined sugar and a return to organically-grown produce. In the 1940s, '50s and '60s, his was a voice in the Perthshire wilderness. His exhortations to people to eat wholemeal bread led to the baker in Aberfeldy producing what became known as 'the doctor's loaf', because it was so unusual. Prophets are rarely honoured in their own land but today, as the message sinks in at long last, Dr Yellowlees finds no shortage of converts to his views.

He retraces his research: 'I was very interested in trying to know the cause of diseases. Prevention is a hobby that came about because I spent my time trying to cure. When I came to Aberfeldy in 1948, I was interested in the work of Lady Eve Balfour, an agricultural scientist and practical farmer who, in her book *The Living Soil* suggested that modern diseases were due to food defects. She quoted two researchers in her work: agriculturalist Sir Albert Howard and Sir Robert McCarrison, who looked at medicine, both ecologists interested in the broad background of all living things. There were two features of food quality that were emphasised. Howard talked of the effects of 'organic growing' and postulated that soil fertility is due to the living creatures that inhabit it. He pointed to the artificial chemicals, increasingly used in farming, which disrupted natural processes and made the creatures and plants suffer. He was concerned about the agricultural basis for health.

'McCarrison emphasised the processing by which food is altered. In particular, he said that we take away the vital essence of wheat by making it into white flour. This causes constipation but also removes mineral and vitamins from the wheat. Sugar is a totally concentrated food that is bereft of vitamins so that it is just a fuel. It seemed to me that in this area of the Tay Valley this kind of food was eaten in vast quantities and was the reason why people were so ill. The natural response for me was to encourage people to eat fresh food. Unfortunately, agriculture and commerce have moved in the opposite direction. The population of the Tay Valley does not depend on the local produce which is really down to the modern economics of farming. This means that our produce is exported and the food that we eat is imported. Fresh food is vitally important for health. The only way for me to get fresh vegetables is to grow them myself in my garden. For a time I ran a market garden near the Tay; I never used any toxic sprays and found myself with a good supply of food. The strath near to Aberfeldy is good land and would be excellent for growing vegetables. But most people seem to get their vegetables from supermarkets. There obviously isn't a market for just local fresh food – the units and economies of selling are too large for that.'

Dr Yellowlees laments the passing of a way of life which saw local folk closer to nature, albeit closer to the poverty line as well. 'It is an awful shame that there isn't a viable market garden in this area, but it would be too much to ask to turn the clock back. It's the same with dairy products – at one time there were at least six dairies around Aberfeldy but now there are none. These trends have added to the depopulation of rural areas. In 1948 I used to go to many small family farms but these are all too rare now. So, non-fresh food has an effect on population as it does with health. My practice went as far as Killin to the west and down to Ballinluig. In 1948 there were ten primary schools and I reckon that there are half that number now. I appreciate that many people were glad to escape from a hard life on the land but I find it sad nonetheless. It is sad that rural communities were not able to take advantage of the richness of their own produce. I think that rural life definitely had advantages for people's well-being, as they were at one time more in touch with nature in all its forms. It was a real world where families were raised in tandem with the disciplines of farm life. Natural food was part of the culture and I am pleased that there has been a move towards returning to "healthfood".'

The population in the area around Aberfeldy may have declined over the years but there is no disputing the community spirit of a small town at the very heart of Scotland. Although conservation-minded, local folk are also keen to develop opportunities for tourism and trade. That means that the community is alive with ideas and there is occasionally controversy about the way ahead. A significant boost to the cohesion of the community has come with the advent of Heartland FM, Britain's smallest commercial radio station. It is largely run by volunteers and broadcasts only at the weekends, but it has brought radio to some parts of Perthshire for the first time and attracts a fierce loyalty from its listeners who really do regard Heartland FM as their own radio station. Sarah Bull, the station's administrator and only paid employee, explains. 'The station serves a 30-mile radius which includes Aberfeldy, Kenmore and Dunkeld as well as Pitlochry. Heartland FM is a voluntary station that is run by people in the community and we are the smallest independent radio station in Britain. It was an idea that began ten years ago and we finally got on air on 21 March 1992. We broadcast on Fridays, Saturdays and Sundays just now but we hope to do weekday breakfast programmes in the future. The funding is raised through advertising but we are not a profit-making organisation. Because the station is a service to the community it is very localised. We don't try to mimic larger stations. Instead, we provide a service for people that is often like a classified ads section in a local newspaper. Our programmes are balanced to 70 per cent speech and 30 per cent music – we don't want wall-to-wall music.

'We do have an obligation in our licence to provide Gaelic programming which we do by broadcasting a Gaelic speech programme. Our programmes are quite light but we try to cover as many local issues as possible. The programme *Roots*, for instance, looks at local issues with an invited panel of guests, and things often get quite heated. There are probably over a

Taymouth Castle

Loch Tay from Kenmore

hundred volunteers who contribute to the station. All the technical work is carried out on a voluntary basis. Many people come in and they end up doing what they are best at.

'We broadcast to around 5,500 people and double that number during the summer. We do special "What's On" programmes in the summer on Fridays to keep visitors informed, and we are very much a local noticeboard of the airwaves.'

Brendan Murphy, Aberfeldy-based director of Heartland FM, has been with the tiny station since its inception. 'The station actually reaches a much bigger audience than we anticipated and we do have quite a few listeners in Perth and Bridge of Earn. We have had a good response from advertisers in Perth. Ultimately we will be moving into whole week broadcasting, but we've got to crawl before we can walk.'

The history of the land around Aberfeldy is the stuff of myth and legend. From the battlements of Garth Castle the feared Wolf of Badenoch cheerily pushed prisoners to their death below. In the woods and humble cottages above the Tay the outlawed Rob Roy MacGregor led his persecutors a merry dance. At Fortingall King Metallanus ruled from 10 BC to AD 29 and welcomed Roman envoys sent by Caesar Augustus. One of these is said to have had a son to a local woman and the myth of Pontius Pilate being born by the Tay was born. Remarkably, there is a living, if silent, witness to these events in the shape of a 3,000-year-old yew tree, Europe's oldest piece of vegetation, in the churchyard at Fortingall. This land was the traditional territory of the Clan Menzies and at Castle Menzies in Weem, just outside Aberfeldy on the north bank of the Tay, the clan still holds its annual gathering. A display inside the house tells the 400-year history of what is a Z-plan tower house of a sort unique to the East of Scotland. It was in this peaceful parish of Weem that the Gaelic-speaking Highlanders launched their last rebellious bid for freedom – not in 1745 but more than 50 years later, when the United Scotsmen, inspired by the French Revolution, launched a call to arms. More than 16,000 are said to have answered the call issued by Angus Cameron and James Menzies, the local leaders of the revolutionary society. In 1797 the Highlanders rose not to promote the dynastic aspirations of distant aristocrats but in defence of their own rights. The people's army captured Menzies Castle and cleared out the armoury of Taymouth Castle, before marching on Blair Castle where they made a prisoner of the Duke of Atholl. The short-lived revolt ended with the arrival of troops; Cameron and Menzies were able to flee to America but things would never be the same again. Notice had been served that feudalism's time was up.

The powerful land-owning families of the Scottish Highlands still held considerable sway but their ascendancy was no longer guaranteed. The grand palace of Taymouth Castle, the former home of the Earls of Breadalbane and once considered by Queen Victoria as an alternative to Balmoral, is a monument to the passing of aristocratic splendour. From here the Breadalbanes controlled an empire which stretched for a hundred miles and, even in this century, extended to 400,000 acres. The Breadalbanes passed into history in the 1920s but they have left a mark at Taymouth and Kenmore, the model village situated at the entrance to the rolling parkland of Taymouth. The Kenmore Hotel is reputed to be the oldest tavern in Scotland, having been founded in 1572 by Sir Colin Campbell, a direct ancestor of the Breadalbanes. Here the Tay salmon season is ritually opened each January and weary travellers have rested and enjoyed Highland hospitality for centuries. One of them, an early graffiti artist by the name of Robert Burns, left a poem penned above the fireplace which can still be read. Little has changed since the Bard described the spectacle of the Tay beginning its long journey that has enthralled generations:

> The outstretching lake, embosomed 'mong the hills,
> The eye with wonder and amazement fills;
> The Tay meandering sweet in infant pride,
> The Palace rising on its verdant side,
> The lawns, wood fringed in Nature's native taste,
> The hillocks dropped in Nature's careless haste;
> The arches striding o'er the newborn stream;
> The village glittering in the noontide beam.

Here the Tay emerges from its huge natural reservoir which drains the hills of Perthshire and mountains of Argyll. Sixteen miles to the west, Loch Tay welcomes the Dochart and the Lochay at lovely Killin. The bridge over the Tay at Kenmore is the first of 20 man-made crossings over Scotland's mightiest river. It is said to be at the very heart of Scotland; what is more certain is that it is a special place in the hearts of many Scots.

Appendix I

HISTORIC BUILDINGS AND PLACES

ABERNETHY

On A913, 8 miles SE of Perth

Unspoilt conservation village, an important Pictish settlement. Featuring the eleventh-century **Abernethy Round Tower**, 74ft high, and one of only two such surviving towers in Scotland. Open daily Monday–Saturday 10 a.m.–5 p.m., Sunday noon–5 p.m.

BALMERINO ABBEY

In the lovely village of Balmerino, near the Tay, this thirteenth-century Cistercian abbey suffered during the Reformation.

CLAYPOTTS CASTLE

Arbroath Road, Dundee

A fine Z-plan sixteenth-century tower house. Standing four storeys high and with an oblong keep, two round towers at the corners retain their original gun ports.

RRS DISCOVERY

Discovery Point, Dundee
Tel. (0382) 201245
Open from 10 a.m. Monday–Saturday (from 11 a.m. on Sundays); last admission 5 p.m. Closed 25 December, 1 and 2 January
Admission charge

Captain Scott's vessel which took him to the Antarctic, the Royal Research Ship is now among the most popular attractions in Dundee. Built in the city in 1901, the ship's return in 1986 marked a significant point in Dundee's revitalisation. The vessel is now berthed at a new dock by the Tay beside a purpose-built visitor centre.

DUDHOPE CASTLE

Dudhope Park, Dudhope Street, off Lochee Road, Dundee

Home of the Constables of Dundee from the thirteenth century. In the eighteenth century it contained a woollen mill and later became a barracks. Bought by the city in the late 1800s, the castle has now been renovated into flats and offices. It has been the backdrop for a number of Dundee's community dramas over the last few years.

Balmerino Abbey

DUNKELD CATHEDRAL

Open all year

Set in beautiful parkland beside the River Tay, the cathedral's remains are a magnificent reminder of Dunkeld's historic position as the ecclesiastical capital of Scotland.

DUNKELD LITTLE HOUSES

Cathedral Street, Dunkeld

Dating from 1689 these houses have been restored to their former glory by the National Trust for Scotland. They now contain a tourist information centre, including video presentations.

FAIR MAID'S HOUSE

North port, Perth
Tel. (0738) 25976
Open Monday–Saturday, 10 a.m.–5 p.m.

Former home of Catherine Glover, heroine of Sir Walter Scott's *Fair Maid of Perth*. Now a craft centre.

THE FRIGATE UNICORN

Victoria Dock, Dundee
Tel. (0382) 200900
Open all year
Admission charge

The oldest British-built warship afloat, the *Unicorn* is now a museum. The 46-gun wooden frigate was launched in 1824, and now contains historical artefacts from its long history.

LINDORES ABBEY, NEAR NEWBURGH

Remains of the once-important twelfth-century Benedictine abbey often visited by Scottish kings.

MAINS OF FINTRY CASTLE

Caird Park Dundee, off Kingsway

The home of the Graham family of Fintry until the early seventeenth century, the castle is now a popular restaurant set in one of the city's liveliest parks.

ST JOHN'S KIRK

Perth City Centre, between High Street and South Street

A magnificent cruciform church dating largely from the fifteenth-century. It was the scene of John Knox's momentous sermon of 1559.

ST MARY'S CHURCH, GRANDTULLY

Off A827, 2 miles ENE of Aberfeldy at Pitcairn Farm
Open all year

A sixteenth-century church with a remarkable painted ceiling. Key available at the farm any time during the day.

ST MARY'S PARISH CHURCH AND TOWER

High Street, Dundee

Open Monday, Tuesday, Thursday and Friday 9 a.m.–noon

Dundee's oldest surviving building, the 'Old Steeple' was built in the fifteenth century and restored last century. The tower affords magnificent views of the city centre and the river.

ST PAUL'S CATHEDRAL

High Street, Dundee

Built in 1853 on the site of the medieval Castle of Dundee, this is an example of the work of Sir George Gilbert Scott. The tower and spire reach 210ft into Dundee's skyline. The cathedral is open daily and features stained glass mosaics and a beautiful reredos by Salviati of Venice.

VERDANT WORKS

West Henderson's Wynd, Dundee, just west of city centre

For further information and opening times, phone (0382) 26659

A nineteenth-century flax and jute mill now being restored to become a living museum of Dundee's textiles industries.

WADE'S BRIDGE, ABERFELDY

Dating from 1733, this famous bridge was designed by William Adam and proved vital as a crossing of the Tay for General Wade's network of roads. Nearby is the Black Watch memorial.

Appendix II

CASTLES AND STATELY HOMES

BALLINBREICH CASTLE
The proud remains of this fourteenth-century castle can be seen close to the River Tay at Newburgh.

BLAIR CASTLE
Off A9, 6 miles NW of Pitlochry
Tel. (0796) 481207
Open daily April–October
Admission charge
A white-turreted castle, seat of the Duke of Atholl. Noteable collections of furniture, pictures, embroidery, arms and porcelain. Extensive grounds, nature trail, deer park, restaurant, shop and caravan park.

ELCHO CASTLE
4 miles SE of Perth, via road to Rhynd
Admission charge
This ancestral seat of the Earl of Wemyss is notable for its tower-like wings or jambs.

HUNTINGTOWER CASTLE
Off A85, 3 miles NW of Perth
Fifteenth-century castellated mansion, known as Ruthven Castle until 1600. Fine painted ceilings.

CASTLE MENZIES
On B846 to Weem, 1 mile W of Aberfeldy
Tel. (0887) 820982
Open daily April–mid October
Admission charge
Sixteenth-century Z-plan fortified house, under restoration by Menzies Clan Society. Tearoom.

Balhousie Castle, home to the Black Watch Museum

SCONE PALACE

Off A93, 2 miles NE of Perth
Tel. (0738) 52300
Open daily March to October
Admission charge

Home of the Earl of Mansfield, the Stone of Destiny was brought here in the ninth century before being taken to Westminster Abbey by Edward I. The house contains fine collections of furniture, needlework, clocks and ivories. Restaurants.

The grounds are the location of Moot Hill, the crowning place of Scottish kings. Also contains an adventure playground, Highland cattle, peacocks and pinetum.

Appendix III

MUSEUMS, ART GALLERIES AND PLACES OF INTEREST

ABERFELDY MALT WHISKY DISTILLERS
Tel. (0887) 820330
Open all year; phone to confirm opening times
Free guided tour and single malt tasting. Shop.

ABERFELDY WATER-MILL
Mill Street, Aberfeldy
Tel. (0887) 820803
Open daily end March–end October; phone to confirm opening times
Admission charge
A restored working oatmeal water-mill. Audio-visual presentation, tea-room, craft shop.

BORELAND RIDING CENTRE
Fearnan, Lochtayside, by Aberfeldy
Tel. (0887) 830212
Horse-riding, trekking, rally-karting. Advance booking is advisable.

BROUGHTY CASTLE MUSEUM
Castle Green, Broughty Ferry, Dundee
Tel. (0382) 76121
Open all year; phone to confirm opening times
A fifteenth-century estuary fort located by the shores of the Tay. Beseiged by the English in the 1500s and attacked by Cromwell's army under General Monck in the seventeenth-century. Now a museum with displays on local history, arms and armours, seashore life and Dundee's whaling history.

BLACK WATCH MUSEUM
Balhousie Castle, Hay Street, Perth
Tel. (0738) 21281 ext 8530
Open all year; phone to confirm times
Many relics illustrating the story of the world-renowned Black Watch regiment.

CAITHNESS GLASS
Inveralmond, A9 1 mile N of Perth on city bypass
Tel. (0738) 37373
Open all year; phone to confirm opening times
Factory shop and restaurant, glassmaking visitor centre, carpark, tourist information centre.

CHILDHOOD HERITAGE CENTRE
Cuil-an-Daraich, Logierait (on A827 E of Ballinluig)
Open Easter to Christmas
Admission charge
Extensive collection of toys and displays relating to a child's life between the wars. Tea-shop, shop, gardens.

DUNDEE REP THEATRE
Tay Square, Dundee
Tel. (0382) 23530
Dundee Repertory Theatre stages drama, music and entertainment. The impressive building also houses a café-bar, restaurant and visual arts gallery. Contact box office for programme details.

FAIRWAYS HEAVY HORSE CENTRE
Off A85 at Kinfauns, 2 miles E of Perth
Tel. (0738) 25931
Open daily April–September; phone to confirm opening times
Clydesdale demonstrations, foals, vintage implements, video shows.

GLENGOULANDIE DEER PARK
By Aberfeldy
Tel. (0887) 830306
At the foot of Schiehallion, the deer park features a fine herd of red deer and a white stag. Also to be seen in this 'drive-through' attraction are Highland cattle, geese, mallard and muscovy ducks, and rare breeds of sheep and goats.

THE HOWFF
Meadowside, Dundee city centre
An historic graveyard which was formerly the garden of Greyfriars Monastery, gifted to the people of Dundee by Mary, Queen of Scots. Until 1778 it was the meeting place of the Nine Trades of Dundee and the signs and symbols of the old craft guilds can be seen on the great variety of gravestones.

LOCH OF THE LOWES
Off A923, 2 miles NE of Dunkeld
Tel. (0350) 727337
Osprey nests and wildfowl may be watched from the hide. Wildlife exhibition and tape/slide programme at visitor centre (Scottish Wildlife Trust).

LOCH TAY POTTERY

Fearnan
Tel. (0887) 830251
Open daily
Pottery workshop and showrooms. Pottery demonstrations by arrangement.

McMANUS GALLERIES

Albert Square, Dundee
Tel. (0382) 23141 ext 136
Open all year
Victorian Gothic building was built in 1867 to Sir George Gilbert Scott's design. The art collection includes fine examples of nineteenth and twentieth-century Scottish paintings, drawings, sculpture, furniture, clocks, glass, ceramics and silver.

The human history collection relates life in Tayside from prehistoric times through to the Industrial Revolution and right up to the twentieth century. The archaeology gallery has a significant display from Ancient Egypt.

MILLS OBSERVATORY

Balgay Hill, Dundee, 2 miles W of city centre
Tel. (0382) 67138 to confirm opening times
Constructed in 1935 for the people of Dundee, the Mills Observatory is Britain's only full-time public observatory. It houses a 10-inch refracting telescope. During the winter viewing the night sky is possible under the supervision of the resident astronomer. Also gives panoramic views over the Tay to Fife.

PERTH MUSEUM AND ART GALLERY

George Street, Perth
Tel. (0738) 32488
Open all year, Monday–Saturday
Fine art, applied art, award-winning natural history gallery and local history gallery.

PERTH THEATRE

High Street, Perth
Tel. (0738) 21031
Beautifully restored repertory theatre. Contact box office for programme details. Exhibitions, restaurant, bar and coffee bar.

MUSEUM OF THE SCOTTISH HORSE REGIMENT

The Cross, Dunkeld
Open daily Easter–end September (closed Tuesday and Wednesday)
Admission charge
Collection illustrating the Regiment's history.

SEAGATE GALLERY
36-40 Seagate, Dundee
Tel. (0382) 26331
Contemporary art exhibitions.

SHAW'S DUNDEE SWEETIE FACTORY
Fulton Road, Wester Gourdie Industrial Estate, Dundee (off Kingsway)
Tel. (0382) 610369
Phone to confirm visiting times
Sweetie-making machinery dating from 1936 to 1956, all restored to its original condition. Confectionery made using recipes dating back to 1879. Viewing area and a chance to taste sweets from a bygone era.

TOURIST ISLAND
Off A9 at Bankfoot, 8 miles N of Perth
Tel. (0738) 87696
Open all year; phone to confirm opening times
Admission charge
Motor Museum, shop and restaurant.

TULLOCHVILLE FARM HEAVY HORSE CENTRE
Tullochville Farm, Coshieville, by Aberfeldy
Tel. (0887) 830365
Clydesdale horses and implements used to farm the land; harnesses and memorabilia.

UNITED AUCTIONS LTD
Perth Agricultural Centre
Tel. (0738) 26183
Livestock market. Sales Monday and Friday from 11 a.m. approx. A focal point of local farming life. Visitors welcome.

Appendix IV

PARKS AND GARDENS, WALKS AND TRAILS

BALGAY PARK
Blackness Road, Dundee
Large park and wood, containing a 9-hole golf course, putting greens, tennis courts and a children's play area. Balgay Hill makes for a pleasant wooded walk and at the summit is the Mills Observatory. Also includes one of the city's oldest and most fascinating cemeteries.

BEATRIX POTTER GARDEN
Birnam Institute, Station Road, Birnam
Garden which celebrates the famous children's writer's associations with the Perthshire village. Features sculptures of her best-loved characters and a children's rabbit warren.

BELL'S CHERRYBANK GARDENS
Off Glasgow Road, Perth
Tel. (0738) 27330
Open daily May–October
Admission free
Eighteen acres of gardens around the headquarters of United Distillers, incorporating the Bell's National Heather collection. The gardens contain a waterfall, an aviary and a children's play area.

BEN LAWERS VISITOR CENTRE
Off A827, 17 miles SW of Aberfeldy
Tel. (0567) 820397
Admission charge
National Trust for Scotland visitor centre tells the story of Perthshire's highest mountain. Nature trail and hill walk. No coaches.

BIRKS OF ABERFELDY
Off A826 Crieff Road
Carpark and picnic area leads into paths and nature trails through a beautiful wooded den with views of impressive Moness Falls, which was celebrated in verse by Robert Burns.

BIRNAM HILL
Wooded walks include views of River Tay.

BOLFRACKS
On A827, 2 miles west of Aberfeldy
Tel. (0887) 820207
Open daily March—October
Admission charge
A garden for all seasons, containing bulbs, peat walls, herbaceous borders and a stream garden.

BRANKLYN GARDEN
Off Dundee Road (A85) in Perth
Tel. (0738) 25535
Open daily March—October
Admission charge
This National Trust for Scotland garden contains over 3,000 species. Rock gardens, Japanese maples and Himalayan flowers combine in a garden for horticulture enthusiasts and those seeking a peaceful sanctuary.

CAMPERDOWN COUNTRY PARK
3 miles north of Dundee city centre, off the A923
A 520-acre estate with the nineteenth-century Willam Burn Mansion House at its heart. The adjoining woods contain ten miles of walks and trails. Camperdown has horse-riding, an 18-hole golf course and an adventure playground on offer. The Wildlife Centre is open all year, featuring birds and animals from around the globe.

CLATTO COUNTRY PARK
Dalmahoy Drive, Dundee
Tel. (0382) 89076
Comprising 24 acres of water surrounded by footpaths, picnic spots and rambling countryside. Watersports are available beside guided walks and a countryside ranger service.

CLUNY HOUSE
Off minor road, 3 miles NE of Aberfeldy
Tel. (0887) 820795
Open daily March—October
Admission charge
An impressive woodland garden including many rare Himalayan species.

Perth in bloom

DRUMMOND HILL FOREST WALKS
On A827 near Kenmore
Forest walks near the shores of Loch Tay, including a picnic area.

KINNOULL HILL
1 mile east of Perth
Impressive wooded hill overlooking the River Tay, with superb views of Fife and Perth. Public park with walks and carparking.

THE LAW
A short journey from Dundee city centre
The plug or core of an extinct volcano forms the highest point in Dundee. Affords magnificent views of the city and the river. Cars and buses can be taken to the summit.

MEGGINCH CASTLE GARDENS
Off A85 between Perth and Dundee
Tel. (0821) 642222
Open Wednesdays and 1–31 August daily
Admission charge
Gardens dating from the sixteenth century. Rose, astrological and walled kitchen gardens.

MONIKIE COUNTRY PARK
About 8 miles NE of Dundee, off the A92. Turn left at the Ardestie crossroads into the B962

Tel. (082 623) 202
Water is the major attraction at this park, 140 acres spread over three water areas. Woodland walks, picnic spots and children's play areas abound.

NORIE MILLER PARK
Queen's Bridge, Perth
A pleasant park which offers good views of the Tay and the city skyline.

NORTH INCH PARK, PERTH
The site of the famous 'Battle of the Clans' in 1396, the North Inch borders on the River Tay. Public playing fields, a golf course, bowling green and children's play area are all contained within its boundaries.

SOUTH INCH PARK, PERTH
A children's fun park and numerous sports facilities are contained in this large public park, only a few minutes from the bustling city centre.

UNIVERSITY OF DUNDEE BOTANIC GARDENS
Riverside Drive, Dundee
Tel. (0382) 66939
Open March–October, Mon–Sat 10.30 a.m.–4.30 p.m., November–February 10 a.m.–3 p.m.
Admission charge
Greenhouses and specially created environments abound in this centre for botanical study.

Appendix V

GAME FISHING
ON THE TAY

Apply for permits, costs and seasons

Loch Tay

BROWN TROUT — J. Lewis, Killin (0567) 820362

SALMON, TROUT — Loch Tay Highland Lodges, Killin (0567) 820323

SALMON, BROWN TROUT, CHAR — Ardeonaig Hotel, South Loch Tayside, by Killin (0567) 820400

BROWN TROUT (north shore) — I. Menzies, Boreland Farm, Fearnan (0887) 830212

SALMON, BROWN AND RAINBOW TROUT (east) — Croft-na-Caber, Kenmore (0887) 830588 or 830236

SALMON, BROWN TROUT — Kenmore Hotel, Kenmore (0887) 830205

BROWN TROUT (and River Tay) — Kenmore Post Office (0887) 830200

River Tay

SALMON, BROWN TROUT (Kenmore) — Kenmore Hotel (0887) 830205

SALMON (Farleyer, near Aberfeldy) — N. A. Hodgkinson, Dunkeld (0350) 728861

BROWN TROUT (Aberfeldy, south bank only) — Jamieson's Sports Shop, 41 Dunkeld Street, Aberfeldy (0887) 820385

SALMON, BROWN TROUT — Weem Hotel, Weem, Aberfeldy (0887) 820381

BROWN TROUT — R. Kennedy, Borlick Farm, Aberfeldy (0887) 820463

SALMON, BROWN TROUT (Derculich Beat, Aberfeldy) — Finlayson Hughes, Estate Office, Aberfeldy (0887) 820904

SALMON, BROWN AND SEA TROUT, GRAYLING (Grandtully, Strathtay) — The Grandtully Hotel, Grandtully, Strathtay (0887) 840207

SALMON, BROWN TROUT (Grandtully Bridge to Tulliepowrie Burn) — Mr Welding, Tulliepowrie House, Strathtay (0887) 840337

SALMON, BROWN TROUT (Edradynate and Upper Grandtully) — Robert Cairns (0887) 840228

SALMON, TROUT (Sketewan) — Mrs Garbutt, Sketewan Farm, Grandtully (0796) 82207

BROWN TROUT, GRAYLING (Kinnaird – Balnaguard – north bank) — Ballinluig Post Office (0796) 482220

BROWN TROUT, GRAYLING (Dalguise and Newtyle beats) — Kettles, Atholl Street, Dunkeld (0350) 727556

SALMON (Dunkeld) — N. A. Hodgkinson, Dunkeld (0350) 728861

SALMON, SEA AND BROWN TROUT, GRAYLING (Hotel Water, Dunkeld) — Stakis Dunkeld House Hotel, Dunkeld (0350) 727771

BROWN TROUT, GRAYLING (Dunkeld south bank) — Kettles, Atholl Street, Dunkeld (0350) 727556

SALMON — M. C. Smith, Burnside, Dalguise, by Dunkeld (0350) 727593

BROWN TROUT (Murthly) — Murthly Post Office (073871) 383; Spittalfield Post Office (073871) 229; A. Deans, 23 Broompark Cres., Murthly (073871) 277

SALMON (Murthly) — The Estate Office, Douglasfield, Murthly (073871) 303

BROWN TROUT, GRAYLING (Meikleour – Luncarty) — Mon–Sat: Stanley Post Office (0738) 828206; Sun: Tayside Hotel, Stanley (0738) 828249

SALMON, SEA AND BROWN TROUT (Benchil, Catholes, Luncarty and Pitlochrie beats) — Tayside Hotel, Stanley (0738) 828249

SALMON (Stanley – Ballathie beat) — Estate office, Ballathie, nr Stanley (025083) 250 or 275

SALMON, SEA, BROWN AND RAINBOW TROUT (lower Scone and Almondmouth beats, Fourdon Loch, Laigh Loch) — Gleneagles Hotel, Auchterarder (0764) 62231

SALMON (lower Scone) — Estate Office, Scone Palace (0738) 52308

BROWN TROUT (lower Scone beat — River Almond) — M. G. Guns & Tackle, 51 York Place, Perth (0738) 25769

SALMON, SEA TROUT (Perth) — Leisure & Recreation Dept., Perth & Kinross District Council, 3 High Street, Perth (0738) 39911

SALMON, SEA AND BROWN TROUT (various stretches) — P. D. Malloch, 259 Old High Street, Perth (0738) 32316

Fishing the Tay

SALMON, SEA TROUT, FLOUNDER (Esturial Water) — City of Dundee District Council, Parks and Recreation Dept., 353 Clepington Road, Dundee (0382) 23141

COURSE FISHING WATERS

Loch Tay

PIKE, PERCH — J. Lewis, Fishing Tackle Shop, Killin (0567) 820362

River Tay

GRAYLING (Grandtully/Strathtay beats) — Mr Welding, Tulliepowrie House, Strathtay (0887) 840337

GRAYLING, PIKE (Sketewan) — Mrs Garbutt, Sketewan Farm, Grandtully (0796) 82207

ROACH (City of Perth Fishings) — Leisure & Recreation Dept., Perth & Kinross District Council, 3 High Street, Perth (0738) 39911

PERCH, ROACH, PIKE, GRAYLING (lower Scone and River Almond) — M. G. Guns & Tackle, 51 York Place, Perth (0738) 25769

GRAYLING, ROACH (various stretches) — P. D. Malloch, 259 Old High Street, Perth (0738) 32316; Kettles, Atholl Street, Dunkeld (0350) 727556

Tay Esturial Water

Dundee District Council (0382) 23141

BIBLIOGRAPHY

John Aitken, *Above the Tay Bridges* (Arthur Gibson, 1986)

Norman Alm (ed.), *Abernyte: Portrait of a Perthshire Village* (Abernyte Press, 1988)

Bill Anderson (ed.), *Royal Tay Yacht Club 1885–1985 Centenary Souvenir* (Burns and Harris, 1985)

Patrick Roger Billcliffe, *James McIntosh Patrick* (The Fine Art Society for Dundee District Council, 1987)

Anthony Burton and John May, *Landscape Detective* (Allen & Unwin, 1986)

A. J. Cooke (ed.), *Baxter's of Dundee* (University of Dundee Department of Extra-Mural Education, 1980)

A. J. Cooke (ed.), *Stanley – Its History and Development* (University of Dundee Department of Extra-Mural Education, 1980)

Ian Crawford, *Held in Trust* (Mainstream, 1986)

Duncan Fraser, *Four Hundred Years around Kenmore* (Standard Press, Montrose, 1972)

Duncan Fraser, *Discovering East Scotland* (Standard Press, Montrose, 1975)

Nigel Gatherer, *Songs and Ballads of Dundee* (John Donaldson, 1986)

Enid Gauldie, *The Quarries and the Feus: A History of Invergowrie* (Waterside Press, 1983)

John Geddie et al, *The River Tay* (T. and A. Constable for the Royal Association for the Promotion of the Fine Arts in Scotland, 1891)

A. R. B. Haldane, *The Great Fishmonger of the Tay – John Richardson of Perth & Pitfour* (Abertay Historical Society Publication No. 21, 1989)

Helen M. Jackson, *A Century of Pastimes and Service* (The Birnam Institute)

S. J. Jones (ed.), *Dundee and District* (British Association for the Advancement of Science, 1968)

Billy Kay (ed.), *The Dundee Book* (Mainstream, 1990)

Maisie Laing, *Your History of Royal Research Ship Discovery* (Pilgrim Press Ltd, 1990)

Bruce Lenman, Charlotte Lythe and Enid Gauldie, *Dundee and its Textile Industry 1850–1914* (Dundee Abertay Historical Society Publication No. 14, 1969)

Kenneth J. Logue, *Popular Disturbances in Scotland 1780–1815* (John Donald, 1979)

Revd Hugh MacMillan, *The Highland Tay* (H. Virtue & Co, 1901)

Lawrence Melville, *Errol: its Legends, Lands and People* (Thomas Hunter and Sons Ltd, 1935)

Lawrence Melville, *The Fair Land of Gowrie* (William Culross and Son Ltd, 1939)

David Paterson, Dorothy Dunnett and Alastair Dunnett, *The Scottish Highlands* (Mainstream, 1988)

Adam Philip, *The Parish of Longforgan* (Oliphant Anderson & Ferrier, 1895)

Adam Philip, *The Songs and Sayings of Gowrie* (Oliphant Anderson & Ferrier, 1901)

John Prebble, *The High Girders* (Martin Secker & Warburg Ltd, 1975)

Mairi Shields, *Newport's Story* (1990)

J. S. Shipway, *The Tay Railway Bridge 1887–1987: a Review of its Origin* (Institute of Civil Engineers, Edinburgh and East of Scotland Association, 1987)

Glyn Slattery, *Trustlands* (Chambers and NTS, 1989)

T. C. Smout, *A History of the Scottish People 1560–1830* (Collins, 1969)

T. G. Snoddy, *'Tween Forth and Tay* (Allen Lithographic Co Ltd, 1966)

Nigel Tranter, *The Fortified House in Scotland: Vol. 2 – Central Scotland* (Oliver and Boyd, 1963)

Norman Watson, *Dundee's Suffragettes* (1990)

West End Community Council, *Magdalen Green Bandstand 1890–1990* (Dundee District Council, 1990)

Hilary Wheater, *Aberfeldy to Glenlyon* (Tamdhu, 1981)

Hilary Wheater, *Kenmore and Loch Tay* (Tamdhu, 1982)

The still waters of Loch Tay

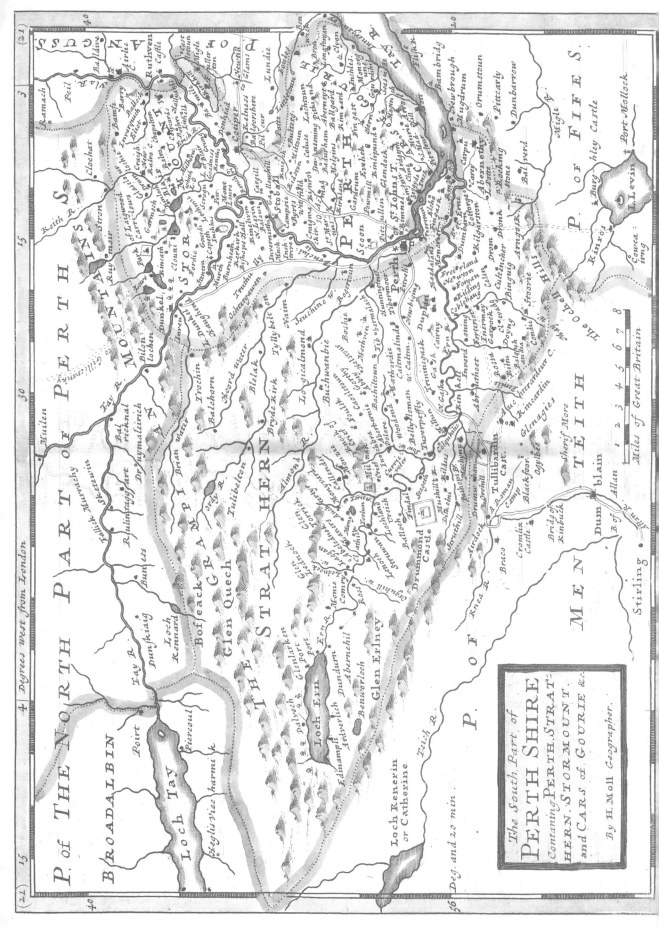

The South Part of
PERTH SHIRE
Contaning PERTH, STRAT=
HERN, STORMOUNT,
and CARS of GOURIE &c.

By H. Moll Geographer.